BOWLING
200+

D0815862

BOWLING 200+

**Mike Aulby and Dave Ferraro
with Dan Herbst**

CONTEMPORARY
BOOKS

CHICAGO

Library of Congress Cataloging-in-Publication Data

Aulby, Mike.
    Bowling 200+ : winning strategies to up your average and
improve your game / Mike Aulby and Dave Ferraro with Dan
Herbst.
       p.   cm.
    Includes index.
    ISBN 0-8092-4338-5
    1. Bowling.   I. Ferraro, Dave.   II. Herbst, Dan.
III. Title.   IV. Title: Bowling two hundred plus.
GV902.5.A85   1989
794.6—dc20   89-9880
                                                 CIP

Copyright © 1989 by Dan Herbst
All rights reserved
Published by Contemporary Books, Inc.
Two Prudential Plaza, Chicago, Illinois 60601-6790
Manufactured in the United States of America
International Standard Book Number: 0-8092-4338-5

BOWLING
200+

Contents

PREFACE

On the surface bowling appears to be such a simple game. You or I roll a ball at a bunch of sticks a mere 60 feet away, and, we hope, they fall down. The concept is so basic and the area so confined that even the rawest of beginners can toss a strike or two.

When we first learn to bowl there is no shortage of instruction. From the printed word to the house pro, we are taught some of the sport's fundamentals. After that, we're on our own.

Except for those who become exceptional players, few of us ever receive further assistance. Despite that, many bowlers progress to realize a modicum of competence. These intermediate-level players average scores of between 150 and 190.

Often we are fooled into *thinking* we know the principles of bowling. As someone who has competed in more leagues than I can count, I can testify to the number of good bowlers whose potential will never be fully realized because of a lack of knowledge. You could be one of them.

In all likelihood, you have all of the physical ingredients

necessary to become a truly outstanding player. But your average has remained frustratingly stagnant, except when a revolutionary new urethane ball hit the market. I'm sure you realize that with good coaching and practice you could really excel.

I'm convinced that virtually all players in the 150–190 scoring category can do better. Much better.

That's why Professional Bowlers Association superstars Mike Aulby and Dave Ferraro wrote this book.

Each of these men is far more than a great player. Both are active teachers of the game with vast experience in transmitting their knowledge to others. They have designed this text specifically for those of you whose needs have been ignored for too long: the better-than-average player.

It's their opinion that most bowlers in the 150–190 average range have developed strong basic skills but are hampered by one or two fundamental flaws in their deliveries. That's why Mike and Dave have gone to great lengths not only to tell you how to bowl, but also to explain the common problems and shortcomings most of us face. They explain how you can analyze and identify flaws and then eliminate them.

I can't think of two better-qualified pros for this project.

Through the first 30 years of the PBA's history, only one man had won both Rookie of the Year and Player of the Year honors. That athlete is Mike Aulby.

He was named top newcomer after his sparkling debut in 1979. Very few freshmen have come close to winning a PBA tournament. Not only did Aulby do that, but he also captured one of bowling's most prestigious events when he beat one of the game's all-time legends, Earl Anthony, 245–217 in the title match for the PBA National Championship.

Six years later Mike became the first professional bowler to top the single-year $200,000 plateau. He did it by winning a half dozen tournaments, including the Brunswick World Open and another PBA National Championship. His selection as that year's outstanding performer was nearly unanimous, the popular Indianapolis native being named on over 80 percent of the ballots. One of the Tour's most fundamentally sound and intelligent performers, Aulby was the runaway leading money-winning southpaw during the 1980s.

In many ways, Dave Ferraro was born to bowl. The son of a proprietor, as a kid he "lived" in Dad's lanes that were next door to the family home. He rolled a 156 at age four and was featured in a national magazine for his skills.

A quarter of a century later, in 1988, he became only the tenth PBA competitor to eclipse the $150,000 plateau. He did it in dramatic fashion, capturing the year's final event when he claimed the top prize of the prestigious Budweiser Touring Players Championship. Ferraro victimized 1986 Bowler of the Year Walter Ray Williams in the deciding game by doubling in the tenth frame to claim a 212–195 decision.

That triumph marked his third win of the year. Remarkably consistent, Ferraro cashed in 20 of 24 events. Had he not been sidelined from several of the PBA's most lucrative Winter Tour stops due to a painful wrist injury, Ferraro might have beaten Brian Voss in his quest to become the first right-handed player in PBA annals to top the $200,000 mark.

Nevertheless, he gained much consolation in knowing that he had established himself as one of the game's most respected performers. His 216.39 average was but 1.65 pins behind pacesetter Mark Roth. Ferraro finished second behind only Voss in voting for the American Bowling Congress's All America Team.

His career wasn't always so successful or profitable. During his early days on tour, Dave fell into a common trap that has claimed many a bowler. He talks candidly in this book about that handicap and how he overcame it to become the star he is today.

You'll learn from these two men the techniques that the top pros use to improve your game. By the time you've reached the back cover you will probably be tired of hearing about "unmuscled" armswings. Yes, we know you won't find *unmuscled* in your dictionary. Despite that, it belongs in your vocabulary for it's one of the key components toward good and consistent shot making.

There are other themes that are mentioned several times. That's not because Dave and Mike have a weakness toward being redundant. It's just that some aspects of bowling are so important—and so often overlooked—that they demand being repeated. It's like knowing what's said to be all that matters in real estate: location, location, and location.

Bowling's keys are a bit more diverse than that. But Mike and Dave realize that it doesn't hurt to harp on the parts of the game that can vastly improve your average. If you find yourself muttering about an "unmuscled" swing in your sleep, you will be well on your way toward reaching your next performance plateau.

As you will soon see, each pro has exclusively authored specific chapters. They assume that you, the reader/bowler, have a basic knowledge of the game's fundamentals. As such, you won't be bored being told how to score, which fingers to place in your ball, or how the pins are numbered.

There are some reference points on which they have assumed you are knowledgeable. They assume that you probably are aware of a lane's geography. If you can't differentiate the tenth board from the third arrow, perhaps a glance at the accompanying "map" will prove helpful (See Diagram 1 in Chapter 1).

For all the outstanding information they present, each man was quick to tell me that the only person who can determine a player's progress is him- or herself. We feel confident that reading the following pages should prove most helpful to your game *if* you hold up your end of the bargain. The road to bowling improvement is the same as that sage advice on how one gets to Carnegie Hall: practice.

In your quest to improve we wish you nothing but good luck and, we hope, a minimum of taps.

Dan Herbst

ACKNOWLEDGMENTS

The authors would like to acknowledge several individuals for their continuous love and support: Jim Aulby; Jo Ann Aulby; Tami Aulby; Jack Ferraro; Lorraine Ferraro; John Ferraro, Sr.; Steve Ferraro; Gloria Ferraro; John David Ferraro; Joseph Herbst; Diane Herbst; Sandy Herbst; Larry Antinozzi III; and Colin Herbst.

We would also like to thank the following people for taking the time to demonstrate bowling skills for the book's photos: Steve Ferraro, Scott Lockshiss, Joe Manniello, and Jim Walsh.

Thanks to photographers Dan Chidester, Frank Valeri and Al Messerschmidt, and to the Professional Bowlers Association for the use of their photographs.

Finally we would like to acknowledge Mid City Lanes, the Showboat Hotel & Casino's Bowling Center, and Showboat's accommodating bowling manager, Jack Cook.

1
THE PRE-SHOT ROUTINE

by Mike Aulby

Good bowling involves repetition. The first-rate player can duplicate the same series of motions time after time to produce consistent shot making. Variety is nice if you're Ed Sullivan or Michael Jordan. For me, I wouldn't mind being able to do the exact same thing one hundred times in a row.

While that's an impossible dream, it is the type of objective for which I strive. Toward that end, I, like virtually all of my fellow professional bowlers, have developed a pre-shot routine.

Prior to beginning my delivery I go through precisely the same series of motions *every* time. This isn't superstition. Rather, it's a group of preparatory activities that put me in the best stead to make a good shot. I want to be physically and mentally set *before* I take that initial step.

The biggest flaws I see with many amateurs are that they aren't mentally ready to bowl when they pick up their ball, and they aren't physically ready to bowl when they begin their delivery. Many players are literally deciding where to aim their shot after they assume their stance.

Having a pre-shot routine that includes concentrating

1

Photo courtesy of the PBA

The top pros, like Mike, are able to repeat good shots.

before you leave your seat is worth quite a few pins to your average.

As I said, 999 out of 1,000 top players have their own unique routines. All good ones, however, contain actions that have an important purpose. They share another common ingredient: consistency.

Whatever you decide to incorporate into your routine, make sure that what you do and the order in which you do it do not vary. If you start doing different things every time, you will find yourself readjusting before every shot. That runs contrary to the purpose of the pre-shot routine.

You want to have the same rhythm, which helps you feel comfortable and confident. After awhile, the routine will become so natural that you do it while on "automatic pilot," thus allowing your mind to concentrate on the task at hand.

I can't count the number of times that fans have asked why I blow into the thumb hole of my ball before placing my hand in it. A lot of it is habit but it does serve a purpose. After wiping resin onto my ball to improve my grip, I find that

Prior to every shot Mike blows warm air into his ball's thumb hole.

Photo by Frank Valeri

blowing into the ball makes the hole warmer. That makes my thumb feel more comfortable. I've been doing that since the early 1980s.

I put the resin into the hole to dry any perspiration that has gotten into the ball. I began blowing it out as a matter of preference. I prefer not to feel the resin on my thumb.

Other bowlers, such as Steve Cook, prefer to leave the resin inside the finger and/or thumb holes. After applying it, Steve rolls his ball inside a towel, since bowling rules stipulate that all foreign substances must be removed from the ball's surface prior to shooting.

Keep your ball clean   Like most players, I thoroughly wipe the surface of my ball before every shot. Failure to do so can allow dirt and lane conditioner (oil) to accumulate. That has the same effect as when the tires of your car hydroplane on a wet road. Your ball will not grip the lane properly and will often skid out of control.

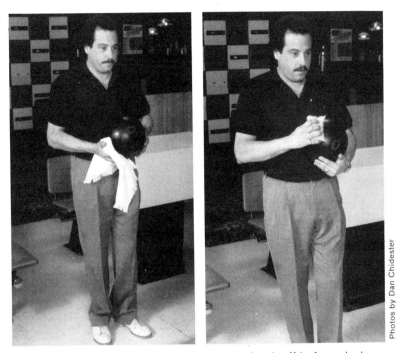

Photos by Dan Chidester

If you pat resin onto your ball be sure to wipe it off before placing your fingers in the holes.

It's tough enough to make a good shot without sacrificing the fruits of a solid delivery because a subtle change in your ball's surface caused it to underreact or overreact. A board or two difference after 60 feet can spell the difference between a split and a double. That's what separates a 155 game from a 185 game.

Reading your ball   In addition, wiping the oil off your ball before every delivery allows you to "read" whether you rolled your previous shot properly. Unless the lanes are as dry as a desert, there will be a ring of oil around your ball. It should appear in the same spot after each strike shot if you are executing a consistent release.

By way of definition, the three different types of rolls can be determined by the location of the oil. If the ring cuts between the finger and thumb hole, you are producing a full roller.

A semiroller sees the track area of the ball a few inches to the outside of the holes (i.e., to the right of the holes on a lefty's ball and on the left side of a right-handed bowler's ball). The ring is a bit closer to the thumb hole than it is to the nearest finger hole (which is the one for your middle finger).

If my track area deviates from the norm, I know my release was altered. If the ring is getting farther away from the finger holes, I know that I've begun to spin the ball or get around the side of the ball (instead of staying behind it) on my release. I might even be doing what is known as "topping" the ball, which is a poor release caused by having the thumb face downward as the shot is made.

Side turn isn't always a negative. There are times when I will intentionally alter my hand position slightly so that I can get the ball to skid through the front portion of the lane before it gets into a roll pattern. The ideal shot is one that skids at first, then rolls, and finally hooks powerfully to explode into the pocket. On very dry lanes the ball can sometimes roll prematurely. When on such a condition, I might opt for more side roll.

Excessive side roll leads to a ball that spins all the way back down the lane. You will find that your shot will lack adequate power. The result is a lot of "weak-hit leaves" such as soft 7 and 10 pins and splits like the 5-10, 5-7, 8-10, and 7-9.

If the track area is too close to the holes then I know I'm coming more directly behind the ball. That means more forward roll, which causes the shot to begin rolling sooner on the lane. That can be either desirable or a disaster, depending on the lane condition. In many cases, an early roll isn't desirable because your ball will "roll out," losing a great deal of its impetus before reaching the pins. On very long oil patterns it could be an asset to get the ball to roll a little bit sooner than normal.

With LDD (limited distance dressing, also known as "short oil") being the condition of choice among most of today's bowling centers, you may not see as definitive an oil ring as in the past. Nevertheless, it's always worth checking, and I highly recommend wiping off your ball before each shot.

The three types of rolls are illustrated here by the track marks they leave behind. The + lines (left) are produced by a spinner, the solid line (center) comes from a semiroller, and the broken line (right) is the result of a full roller.

Doing so also allows you to better read the lane condition. For example, let's say your oil ring is very slight after rolling your strike shots but it's quite pronounced when you convert a 7 or 10 pin. That tells you there is a lot of oil in the middle of the lane. Knowing that cross-lane shots won't hook nearly as much as your strike ball could make the difference between success and failure when you must convert a multiple-pin leave (such as the bucket).

Concentrate Before It's Too Late!

Your pre-shot routine begins before you leave your seat. If you have found the right strike line, you should be thinking about hitting your target. If you have been missing the pocket, you need to determine what move on the lane stands the best chance of being successful. There is no room in bowling for indecision. Make up your mind what you want to do and then concentrate fully on carrying out that plan.

As I stand up, I check the rack of pins to ascertain if

A bowling lane's "geography."

they are all on their proper spots. Some racks are "open," meaning the pocket pins are spread too far apart. The gap between the 1-2 (for a lefty) or the 1-3 (for a righty) needs to be correct.

Unless the pocket pins or the 5 pin are obviously out of place, do not rerack. Otherwise, you'll find that play slows down considerably.

An even more important reason for checking is to make certain that the rack is ready for play. It isn't that unusual for a pin to be missing. You might throw a perfect strike only to have to take the shot over because an opponent noticed that, for example, the 9 pin was AWOL.

On occasion the protective rake hasn't left the lane surface. Rolling a $125 soft urethane ball into a piece of metal isn't something I'd recommend to nonmillionaires.

Prior to stepping onto the approach, check for lane clearance. Simple consideration and etiquette calls for allowing any player on an adjacent lane to complete his or her delivery prior to your stepping onto the approach. In the pros and some top-level amateur events, a two-lane clearance is followed.

My advice to amateurs is to stick with a single-lane policy. That's what I do when I bowl in a local league. Waiting for two lanes on either side to be open makes for very slow bowling.

Taking Control of Your Bowling Ball

Before picking up your ball, make certain that your bowling hand is bone dry. As you use the rosin bag and/or the air blown from the dryer, you can take your first deep breath. Doing so relaxes the body and helps relieve tension.

As I pick up my ball I do so by grabbing it with two hands from its side. I *never* remove the ball from the rack by placing my hand in the holes! Nor do I ever place my hands on the front and the back of the ball where another ball can strike them. I've seen scores of players suffer needless and avoidable injuries when another ball shoots out of the return gate and smashes into their fingers.

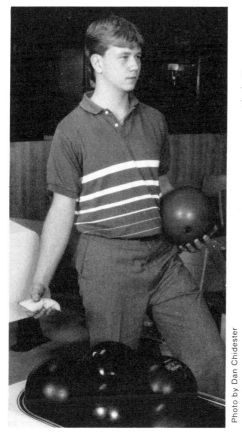

Use a rosin bag and/or the air blower to dry your fingers.

Photo by Dan Chidester

    As you remove your ball from the rack, bend from your knees to help support the weight of the ball. I never lean from my waist to reach across the apparatus to get my ball. You can throw out your back by putting additional stress on your muscles. Remember, even in league play you will be delivering the ball approximately 50 to 70 times. There is always the danger of injuries caused by cumulative muscular stress. Being lazy can be dangerous.

Test That Sliding Shoe

Before I assume my stance, I slide my right foot on the lane (a right-handed player does the same with his left foot). This action isn't a superstition. If a foreign substance has attached

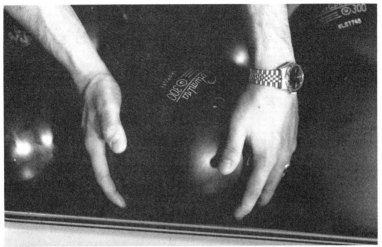

Photo by Dan Chidester

NEVER remove a ball by either putting your hands in front and behind it or grabbing it by the finger/thumb holes.

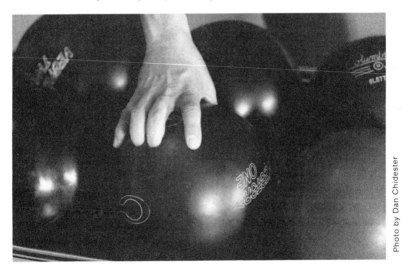

Photo by Dan Chidester

itself to the bottom of my shoe, I don't want to discover it as I fly in midair over the foul line.

That little spill of cola or catsup you stepped in can be disastrous. Unexpectedly, your foot comes to a screeching halt at what should be the start of your slide. Or you might have stepped on some powder and slide clear over the foul line.

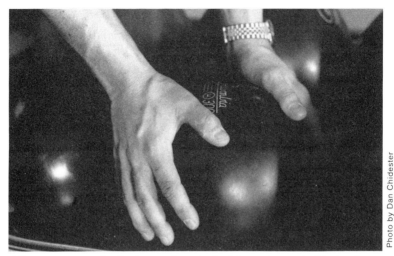

The correct method of removing the ball from the rack. Notice how the hands are placed on either side of the ball.

I've seen a lot of players come back from a shot in pain after sticking at the line. It's something that's pretty tough on the lower back as well as the knees. And, of course, the badly timed foul can cost you a match.

If I'm worried about sliding too much, I will put my ball down and step off of the approach. I'll then use a wire brush to rough up the bottom of my shoe so that the friction between my foot and the approach is increased. A less abrasive way of achieving roughly the same result would be to wipe off the bottom of your shoe with a towel.

In contrast, if I've stepped in something sticky, I will rub cold cigarette ashes into the bottom of my shoe.

By rubbing your sliding foot on the approach you help prevent a buildup of dirt. As the competition progresses, one can visibly detect the approach becoming more dusty. That's especially true in the areas where there isn't as much traffic, such as between lanes. If you step in one of those places a few times your shoe could become more slippery.

Assuming Your Stance

I now place my feet in the predetermined starting position on the approach. As I support the weight of my ball with my

As you step onto the approach, slide your foot on the floor and place it on the proper board.

Photo by Frank Valeri

nonbowling hand I place my fingers into the ball first. After my fingers are comfortably within the holes, I put my thumb into the ball.

I do not know of a single quality player who does not place his hand inside the ball in this order. The fingers always go in first (since they are the last to exit during the release). This also assures that you will achieve the proper and consistent depth for your fingers so that your grip does not vary from shot to shot.

The key is to make certain that your grip is consistent. If you put your fingers at varying distances into the ball you will find that the timing on your release will also vary.

My personal preference is to have my fingers fit loosely. I move my fingers around inside the ball until they feel just right. At that point I will squeeze my thumb into the hole. Keep in mind that while this is the way Mike Aulby likes his grip to feel, you could be just the opposite. Regardless, the finger-first, thumb-second order works best for everyone.

Some athletes "test" their thumb prior to placing their fingers in the ball. They want to make certain that the thumb's size has remained constant. If a change is detected, it may be time to add or remove a piece of tape prior to shooting. When you do this check, place your fingers into the ball first so that you are checking your thumb at the precise position it will be in during your release.

The next stop is to assume your stance. Take a deep breath to help relax your muscles. You are now ready to begin your delivery.

For me, the deep breath is a signal that I'm about to start my pushaway. I raise my ball slowly up to head height before lowering it back to my waist. During that time I am taking that breath. I'm now ready to make my shot.

It's only in recent years that the value of powerfully inhaling has been adequately recognized and appreciated. The proof of how a good breath relaxes a tense body is reinforced every time you see athletes in various sports utilize these techniques to enhance performance. The next time you watch a golfer standing over a putt, a placekicker lined up while awaiting the snap from center, or an NBA player standing at the free throw line, notice how he's likely to take a deep breath before moving into action.

Because my delivery is just as significant and pressure-packed, I do the same. That deep breath helps me to be more fully prepared, mentally and physically, by the time my pre-shot routine concludes.

Notice what I have accomplished in a few seconds of time. My sliding shoe has been found clear of foreign substance, as has my ball. I've "gone to school" by studying the track pattern of the oil before removing it from the ball. My hand and the holes are free of perspiration.

Fast or Slow, It's up to You

Once you have gotten into your stance, it's up to you to determine the amount of time before beginning your delivery. Some players, like Mark Roth, pick up the ball and are gone at a speed that would make A. J. Foyt envious. Others, such as Sweden's Mats Karlsson, are extremely deliberate.

Most of us fall between the two extremes. Conventional wisdom says that waiting too long is a pitfall worth avoiding. Although that works best for people like Mats, it's not what I recommend.

The reason is simple: the longer you stand still, the more rigid your muscles become. Supporting a heavy ball on your arm forces your muscles into action. Remember, ours is a sport in which having a free and unmuscled armswing is vital. Being as loose as possible is the objective.

It's worth noting that Mats has a relatively stiff arm-swing. I'm not sure if that is, in part, due to the length of his pre-shot routine or whether initially having such a swing has told him there is no additional harm done by being so deliberate. However, if your game relies on having an unrestricted armswing, a long wait in your stance will probably prove detrimental.

Besides, the longer you stand still thinking about your shot, the more likely that the anxiety of the moment will overwhelm you. A few seconds at most should suffice for that last deep breath and a mental reminder about what you plan on doing with the upcoming shot.

Mark's get-up-and-go approach is the lesser of those two "evils." Still, I have to feel that it's better to take at least a second or two to clean off your ball and shoes before contemplating the upcoming shot. Don't be haphazard. It's pretty tough to just get up and go and still be able to do everything the same way on a consistent basis.

Having said that, the routines that Mats and Mark use—extreme though they might seem to you or me—are what works best for them. The most important thing in developing your pre-shot pattern is not to copy what the majority of pros do. Instead, do whatever is natural to you. If being like a Roth or a Karlsson is more comfortable to your temperament, by all means that's the way for you to go.

Variety Is the Spice of Bowling Life

There are as many variations to routines as there are bowlers. Steve Cook's trademark is to bounce up and down lightly on his feet as he stands on the approach. He bounces into his first step. Marshall Holman's pace is similar to Mark Roth's. After Marshall puts his hand in the ball he eases down a little bit and relaxes. As soon as he's relaxed, he's gone.

Some players actually look at their ball to see if it's in the proper position. Dave Husted, Wayne Webb, Tom Baker, and Carmen Salvino are prominent pros who employ a visual checklist. I go exclusively by whether I feel comfortable.

There are some bowlers who use mental imagery as a confidence builder at the start of their pre-shot routines. They literally picture themselves making the perfect shot.

That's part of applying full concentration to the task at hand. For example, when I'm in my best groove I don't even notice everyday distractions. Perhaps, during the height of my hot streak in 1985, there was a tornado that ripped through the bowling center. Yours truly probably wouldn't have noticed until pins began flying by my head.

When I'm on my game, nothing can distract me. It's when your concentration waivers that you start noticing the guy on the next lane who is loudly cursing about his lack of luck, the desk telephone that's allowed to keep ringing, or the chap kicking the ball return unit.

If something has caught your eye and broken your concentration, put the ball back into the rack and start your routine all over again.

Mistakes to Avoid

There are a few *don'ts*. Don't scoreboard watch. Either you will put added pressure on yourself to perform or you will think "I only need six pins." When a bowler tries to get only six sticks on a shot, chances are he'll end up with five. It seems you always get one less pin than you want. Indeed, roll every strike ball to the best of your ability.

I can think of but two times when you should be aware of the score. One situation is when you must decide if it's prudent to risk losing wood in an attempt to convert a difficult split. The other is when you need a very small count on your fill ball to win. If your strike line comes dangerously close to the gutter, you should probably roll more directly at the pocket while adding a little ball speed.

Don't rush your shot. There are certain league bowlers who are cutoff specialists. You just know that even if you are on the approach they will start their delivery just after you've begun yours. Don't race through your routine in an effort to shoot before they can. Instead, let them go first so you can take your time in executing a good delivery.

Concentrate on the positive. You might want to remind yourself of how it felt on your most recent good shot. I do not recommend thinking about how to execute your delivery. Unless you are really struggling with your motion, do not tell yourself something like "keep the first step slow and short." Doing so makes it tougher for your delivery to be natural. If you are really having problems, only then should you have such thoughts.

Even when a PBA title is on the line I never think about what's at stake ("Oh, boy, I need to strike to win!") or about what happens if I should fail. Whether we succeed or not, the sun will still be rising in the east tomorrow morning.

A Few Final Thoughts

Most intermediate bowlers know their own game fairly well. In pressure situations your pre-shot routine provides a comforting similarity. That can be a good counterbalance against perceived pressure. What you must do to roll your best shot is exactly the same whether it's in practice or for the U.S. Open title. What makes the latter so much more difficult is that our minds tell us it is. Having the identical pre-shot routine in both extremes is a subconscious reminder that making a game-winning shot is the same as rolling in practice.

In pressure situations, all of us have a "choke tendency." My enemy is trying to "help" and "steer" the ball into the pocket. Having come to recognize that, I now remind myself before a big shot to be disciplined. I concentrate on waiting on my hit so I make a natural shot.

How your pre-shot routine is structured is up to you. The recommendation I offer is to take your ball out of the rack correctly, make certain your hand is dry and your sliding foot's surface is okay, and place your fingers into your ball before your thumb.

Whatever items or idiosyncrasies you add are entirely up to you. However, it is important to have some sort of pre-shot routine whose components are there for a reason. Establishing a consistent rhythm and comforting habits is a big plus.

After a short while, your routine should become second nature. Like shifting gears while driving your car, it's something you're able to do without consciously thinking about it.

2
THE APPROACH

by Mike Aulby

The overwhelming majority of players use either a four- or a five-step approach. The three-step is very rare. The four-step is the most common.

In essence, the five-step approach is really just a four-step delivery with an extra stride at the beginning to get you started.

If you're a smaller person and/or you need to gain more ball speed, you should go with the five-step. So, too, if you aren't able to bowl at least 10 games per week. The less you practice, the more likely that your timing will be the first thing to suffer. It's tougher to maintain consistent timing with four steps than with five.

Regardless of the option that works best for you, some common principles are vital.

Your last (sliding) stride is your longest. It's the natural culmination of a progression in which you make each succeeding step a bit longer and faster than the one before. By doing so you establish a rhythmic tempo as you build momentum. All of your movements should be smooth.

Proper footwork is important. On every step the heel of

your foot should touch the lane first with the toes landing later. Heel-to-toe footwork helps keep your weight back. You will remain more upright from your waist with your knees doing the bending. This helps put you in an ideal position at the foul line to generate maximum leverage which gives your shot added power.

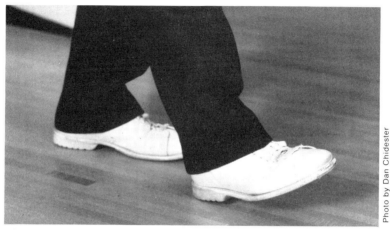

Good footwork is of the heel-to-toe variety.

Photo by Dan Chidester

There are amateurs I've seen who violate these principles. Midway through their delivery they will slow down their feet. Some actually pause for a split second.

Ninety-nine times out of 100, such traits creep into one's game as an inbred physical correction to a timing problem. On the preceding step(s) the player has gotten his footwork ahead of his armswing. The chances are that the flaw can be found in how he puts his feet and the ball into motion. Either the foot movement is early or the ball movement is late.

Since a mid-delivery pause is far from desirable, the best alternative is to work hard on having proper timing at the start of the shot.

The Starting Position

How far back you stand on the approach from the foul line depends on a number of factors. Obviously, a five-step delivery demands more space than does the three-step variety. The bigger you are, the longer your strides. For example, six-foot, seven-inch Steve Cook has often said that he wishes the approach of the lane were two feet longer to accommodate his needs.

The best way to determine your natural starting position is to walk to the foul line and turn your back on the pins. If you are a four-step player, take four brisk walking steps back and then add a half step to allow for your slide. If you are a five-step player, take five brisk strides and then add a half step for your slide. Where you end up is probably the best place to start.

As with all else in bowling, through trial and error you will discover if you need to make a modification. The ideal starting spot is one that leaves your sliding foot an inch or two behind the foul line upon completion of your shot.

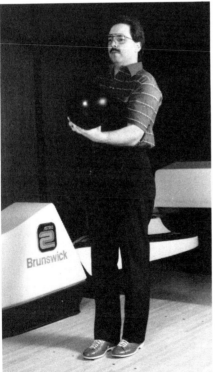

The address position. Notice how Mike holds the ball around waist height and in line with his shoulder as he's properly balanced.

Photo by Frank Valeri

Your starting stance should find your feet parallel or the foot with which you take your first stride a little farther from the foul line. In my case, my left foot is to the side and slightly behind my right.

I suggest holding the ball at waist height with its center in line with the shoulder of your bowling arm. A common shortcoming among many players is a circuitous armswing that begins because the ball is held in the middle of the body during the address. By placing the ball in line with the outside of my body I am able to keep my armswing straight throughout. I use my nonbowling hand to support the weight of my ball before putting it into motion.

Your body faces the pins during your stance with your shoulders square to your target. You should have an upright stance.

If you watch two dozen bowlers you'll probably see 24 different address variations. While there is no "right" or "wrong" starting position it is important that you feel comfortable, have good balance, and have your hand in a natural position on the ball.

Some of those contorted grips that you see among unorthodox players result in added pressure on the muscles at the start, which hinders having a free armswing.

The four-step delivery   After finding a comfortable address position and having completed your pre-shot routine, you are now ready to deliver your shot.

One of the biggest keys in proper execution of the four-step method lies at the start. Your footwork and armswing must begin simultaneously. With the four-step method, a right-handed player starts by striding with his right foot; a left-hander's first step is with his left foot.

For purposes of simplicity, we will refer to this as your starting foot while the opposite foot is the sliding foot. Thus, a left-handed bowler's sliding foot is his right and the right-handed player's sliding foot is his left.

As mentioned, the first step is key. Think of it as your foundation. Just as in building a house, unless your foundation is solid all else will be rendered unsatisfactory. If that first step is too fast your sliding foot will get to the foul line prematurely in relation to your armswing. When it's too slow the opposite could occur.

To build the proper foundation, start with a nice, even walking step. As you do so, the armswing's pushaway occurs. As your foot hits the floor, the ball is extended in front of the side of your body.

A good pushaway is one in which it appears as if you are handing the ball to an invisible person. Extend your arm in front of you so that gravity, not your muscles, will cause the ball to start its descent.

You want the elbow of your bowling arm to be flat. Having a straight arm contributes to having an unmuscled swing.

From this point on, your wrist remains "locked" into the same position. Whether it is cupped, straight, or bent backward, the wrist position must not vary during your delivery.

On step number two the ball will begin to fall as you start your backswing. The ball will be by your side as you complete the stride.

The ball is at the zenith of the backswing on the third step. The height of the backswing varies from player to player. The extremes range from Pete Weber, Amleto Monacelli, and my brother-in-law Steve Cook (who all easily exceed head height) to Del Warren (well below his waist).

In my opinion, the ball should only get as high as it is propelled by a free armswing. By letting the ball swing your arm—not the other way around—your backswing will probably reach roughly shoulder height.

Ideally, your final step will find you in perfect time. You will be finishing your slide as your hand is releasing your shot and your sliding foot is pointed directly ahead.

The five-step delivery   Most accomplished pros can use either the four- or five-step method. In fact, George Pappas won the 1979 Firestone Tournament of Champions the first week after changing from a four- to a five-step delivery. The reason he made that adjustment was that he had been experiencing timing problems.

Photo by Frank Valeri

Consistent timing is critical. In a four-step delivery the first stride coincides with the pushaway.

It is easier to be in time with the addition of the extra step. The only difference between the two techniques is that the five-step approach sees you putting the ball into motion on your second stride.

The initial step tends to be very short and slow. Its purpose is just to get you moving. As you begin the second step the ball is pushed forward. From then on everything is identical to the four-step delivery.

Timing

There are players who have "early" or "late" timing, meaning that their release either precedes or follows their slide.

Photos by Frank Valeri

The ball is at the player's side on the second step and at the zenith
of the backswing during the succeeding stride.

As the sliding foot approaches the foul line the downswing nears its conclusion. A good release follows as you are well balanced, thanks to a good knee bend.

Of bowlers who are out of time, most men tend to be early while the majority of women are late (this may also hold true for getting ready for a night out on the town, but I'll leave that issue to other authors).

Early timing occurs when you release your shot before completing your slide. The result is that you don't take full advantage of the power in your sliding leg, which causes you to sacrifice leverage. Very often, your swing is excessively

Early timing sees the ball get to the line before your sliding foot. As one glance renders obvious, this technique robs you of much-needed leverage.

Photo by Dan Chidester

muscled and you have too much ball speed. The end product sees you leaving a lot of the so-called "weak hits" such as soft 7 (for lefties) and 10 pins (for righties) and/or 5 pins.

Late timing sees your slide end before you let go of the ball. Very often the shot is then dropped downward into the lane. This, too, results in lost power.

When a player is out of time, his shot may also stray from its intended target. An early release can cause you to pull the ball. Hopefully, you'll get lucky and cross over to the Brooklyn side. As often as not, your shot will strike the nose of the headpin and you'll be left with a split. The late release could cause you to be light or miss the entire headpin (a southpaw would be wide to the left of the pocket).

There are several power players who are intentionally late. By planting their sliding foot before their release they can obtain greater leverage. This method requires significant strength since the arm must carry the ball through the downswing after the opposite foot has come to a halt. This tends to result in a "muscled" delivery which runs against current conventional wisdom.

Other negatives of intentional late timing are that accuracy and necessary ball speed are more difficult to achieve. To perfect this method, you probably must make a commitment to bowl a significant number of games on a regular basis. You also need uncommon arm strength. Because of the accuracy/ball speed problems, late timing is a technique that I don't recommend for nonprofessional players.

The more you are able to practice, the less of a handicap late timing becomes. However, my sentiments are not necessarily gospel. Dave has a different perspective. When he was developing his game, Dave's father taught him to plant his sliding foot before releasing his shot to gain power.

I'm convinced the most important ingredient concerning your timing is consistency. If you are late or early on each shot your armswing can adjust. Mark Roth has won 30 plus titles and over $1 million while being "late" with every delivery.

Which brings us to an important point. The star who doesn't go by the book is described as being "unorthodox." The struggling player who is unorthodox is thought to suffer from having major flaws in his game.

There is an axiom in bowling that what counts isn't "how" but "how many." This applies to timing. The bowler who really struggles is the one who is in time on one shot,

In contrast, Dave's plant and shoot method allows him to fully utilize his leg strength to impart added power to his shot.

Photo by Dan Chidester

early the next, and then late the shot after that. He'll do more spraying than an exterminator!

By getting to that foul line the same way on shot after shot, you may not need to change your game just to become a textbook player. On the other hand, if your carry percentage on pocket hits isn't what it should be, then you should consider experimenting with your timing.

If you wish to correct early timing, slow down the ball movement on your first step. Another option is to push the ball out and slightly upward. Conversely, if you are always late, try putting the ball into motion a fraction of a second before your footwork commences.

Leverage

If you follow the sport closely, you are probably aware that most pros consider keeping their legs in shape to be their number one physical fitness priority. That's because the sliding leg that is conditioned and in proper position upon a shot's release is a great asset when it comes to generating striking power.

The ideal release position sees the player bending from the knees and *not* from the waist. Doing so allows you to shoot the ball onto the lane, not into it. Bowlers who bend from the waist have their shots "roll out" by the time they have reached the pins. Their hook may look pretty, but the majority of the power of their shot has been expended before their ball reaches the pins.

Stand fairly upright throughout your delivery. As your final step concludes, the knee on your sliding leg is either in line or a bit farther forward than your shoulders.

While a good knee bend is important, you don't want to overdo it. A bend that's excessive forces you to bend the elbow of your bowling arm. The ideal release position is such

As you release your shot it's very helpful to have a good knee bend that is achieved by your knee being farther forward than your shoulders.

Photo by Dan Chidester

that the bottom of the bowling ball is roughly six inches above the floor when held by your straight arm.

You want to release your shot with the ball within inches of the ankle of your sliding foot. Believe it or not, the pros with exceptional leverage tend to have more accidents in which the ball strikes their ankle than does a mediocre player. That's because the distance between the ball and their ankle is so slight.

There have been weeks when I have hit my ankle a half dozen times during the course of a tournament. When that happens you'd be amazed how good an ice pack can feel! Like all other parts of the game, you can't be intimidated by the thought of that occurring any more than a baseball hitter could allow himself to worry about fouling a fastball off of his toes.

The greater the distance from sliding ankle to the ball, the less leverage you will obtain. In addition, you'll have a tendency to "circle" the ball in an attempt to pull it toward your target. This will cause you to come around the side of the ball, which sees your ball having too much spin and not enough of a powerful roll.

While the ball should be close to your ankle, there should still be a gap of a few inches between the two. Otherwise, you'll find yourself pushing the ball out toward your target.

The Armswing

Bowling is one of the rare sports in which there are aspects of the game in which an athlete makes a concerted attempt *not* to utilize his muscle power. The best armswing is one in which the ball guides the arm, not the other way around.

The straighter the swing, the better. Bowlers with slender hips have a distinct advantage in that they don't have to loop the ball around their body. By being able to maintain a straight swing throughout, they avoid having to use muscle as well as having to align before realigning their arm.

I like to think of my arm as a string with my shoulder as the fulcrum. As a left-handed player I place the ball in front of the left side of my body on the first step and let gravity do the rest. I try never to "force" the ball to obtain a higher or shorter backswing.

Ideally, I want the ball to travel in a straight line. Many amateurs have loops in their armswings in which the ball either travels behind their back or well off to the side. That's dangerous. With a circuitous armswing, they must release the ball at the precise moment in order to hit their target. If their sliding foot is either late or early, the shot will be well off-line.

On the other hand, a straight armswing allows one to overcome slight timing deficiencies more easily.

The Release

One aspect of the game that really separates the exceptional from the mediocre player is the quality of the hand release. You need to develop an excellent release if you are to become an exceptional bowler.

Many amateurs "top" their shots by having their thumb face the floor as they let go of the ball. Others "spin" their shots by coming completely around the ball. Both of these techniques are wrong.

I keep my hand "locked" into the same position throughout my delivery until my release. In most cases, my thumb can be found somewhere between the ten and eleven o'clock positions. The right-handed player would have his thumb between one and two o'clock.

Make sure to conclude your shot with a straight follow-through. As you do so, reach out as if to "grab" your target.

There are two adjustments that dictate how much your ball will hook. One way is to switch bowling balls. The other method is to alter your hand release position. The former is definitely easier, especially if you don't bowl the great volume of games that pros do. Nevertheless, I prefer to switch hand positions if given the choice.

If I want the ball to roll a little sooner I will opt for increasing my forward roll (in which the ball rolls end-over-end). I accomplish that by turning my thumb toward one or

Upon releasing the ball the thumb exits first to allow the fingers to impart lift. This can only occur if your hand is locked into the proper position.

Photo by Dan Chidester

two o'clock (ten to eleven for a right-handed player). I "lock" into that position throughout, gripping my ball almost as if it were a suitcase. The shot will then roll sooner and go straighter.

There are times when you will want more side turn so your ball will skid through the head area of the lane and finish with a sharper and more powerful break at the end. With ten to eleven o'clock as your starting position, you rotate your hand either clockwise (for us lefties) or counterclockwise (for right-handed players). This twisting motion begins at the bottom of your swing, just before you release your shot.

As you let go with your shot, the thumb moves upward toward the noon position. If my thumb was at ten o'clock before, it will move to eleven on my release and conclude at noon when my follow-through is done. Make sure to come *around* the ball and not over it.

Regardless of which type of roll I'm attempting, I always want to hit *through* the ball on my release. Do not try to hit up or down on the ball. If you throw it downward the ball will go into the lane and lose power. If you throw it upward the ball will hook early and will have run out of steam by the time it reaches the pins.

The key words to remember are *through* and *out* (toward the pins).

If everything that precedes it is correct, you should produce a good follow-through. Except for the side turn shot, you should not make any attempt to have your hand rotate around the ball. The way that we are built will allow you to get necessary lift and turn on the ball simply by coming straight through your shot. Do not force the issue!

Wrist Positions

Another way of altering the amount that your shot hooks is by changing your wrist position. If you "cup" your wrist the ball will hook earlier and a lot more. To delay and minimize hook, break your wrist backward. Keeping your wrist in a flattened (straight) position allows for a hook that falls between the two extremes.

Regardless of which option you select for a shot, make certain to maintain the same wrist position throughout the entire delivery. Pretend that a hard cast had immobilized your wrist into one set position.

If these adjustments don't come naturally, you might try a wrist support device that does the work for you (see Chapter 6). My personal preference is to keep my wrist unencumbered. By doing so, I can make a last-second adjustment with my wrist to increase or decrease the hook. However, that's an advanced technique and one that's best left to us pros.

Lofting shots   If you are hitting the pocket but not carrying, rollout could be your problem. That occurs when your ball expends a great (and unnecessary) amount of its energy getting through the conditioner that's found on the heads of

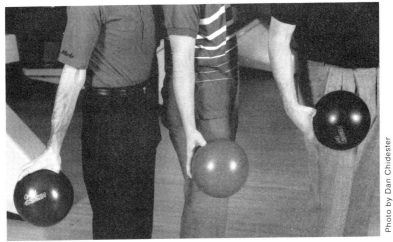

Photo by Dan Chidester

The three wrist positions are (from left to right): bent backward, to "kill" hook; normal; and cupped, to promote hook.

the lane. By the time your ball hooks, much of its power is gone.

Negating the heads is everyone's goal, but few bowlers are completely successful. Two of the best are Mark Roth and Dave Ferraro. Both loft their shots.

It isn't necessary to throw the ball halfway down the lane on the fly to beat the oil pattern. Just hit through on your shot so that it gets a foot or two over the line. Make sure that you release the ball as it is moving parallel to the floor. You want it to move outward. Never lose the ball on the down--swing or toss it as your hand is moving upward.

The amount of loft varies based on the lane condition. The drier the head area, the earlier your shot will hook. To avoid rollout and to obtain the desired skid-roll-hook pattern, utilize maximum loft. On the other hand, very oily heads might call for employing little or no loft.

On the PBA Tour the lanes are oily during morning blocks and drier in the evenings. Unless you are familiar with the maintenance schedule of the center in which you are bowling, you will need to discover the lane condition as you compete.

This is another example of where being observant pays

Photo by Frank Valeri

A good loft helps achieve the desired skid-roll-hook pattern.

dividends. You must watch the ball after it leaves your hand to determine if it's hooking prematurely. That's easier said than done. When using the arrows as your target you will not see your ball until it reaches that portion of the lane. It might be worthwhile to have a knowledgeable teammate observe your shots and you watch his or hers.

Another clue comes from checking the oil ring on your ball before every shot. That can give you a good idea as to the amount of conditioner on the lane.

Ball speed   Rolling a bowling ball at 100 miles per hour, even if humanly possible, would not be to your advantage. Contrary to popular misconception, speed does not equal power.

A ball thrown too fast causes pins to fly over, not into, one another. Instead of the 6 pin taking out the 10 and the 4 hitting the 7, they will fly over them. Ideal speed has them ricochet off the sidewalls and back into play.

On the other hand, a ball that isn't rolled hard enough will not carry the half hits on which pins also deflect off the sidewalls. In addition, it will overreact to the lane conditioner (or lack thereof). Maximum leverage at the point of release yields greater power, not excess ball speed.

What is the optimum speed? It's been my experience on strike balls that anything under 15 miles per hour is too slow and at or above 20 miles per hour is too fast. Somewhere within the 15-19 miles per hour range is a speed that's right for you.

With changing conditions, you may wish to roll the ball a bit faster or slower. As with timing and the release, the key is to obtain a degree of consistency. You can hit your target every time and release the ball the same way, but if your speed varies so will the amount that your shot hooks.

How can you calculate your ball speed? Have a friend use a stopwatch to time how long it takes for the ball to travel from your hand to the headpin. The accompanying chart tells the rest.

BALL SPEED	
Time (in seconds)	Speed (in mph)
4.09	10
3.72	11
3.41	12
3.15	13
2.92	14
2.73	15
2.56	16
2.41	17
2.27	18
2.15	19
2.05	20
1.95	21
1.86	22
1.78	23
1.70	24
1.64	25

If you need to increase your speed, stand farther back on the approach and hold the ball higher during the address point. The higher the ball is held, the faster it will go as gravity forces it to descend. That will result in a bigger backswing. The higher the natural backswing, the more momentum is gained as the ball moves toward the line.

On the other hand, if you wish to slow down, hold the ball lower during the address. If you find yourself leaving a lot of corner pins, try cutting down a little bit on your ball speed.

Photos by Dan Chidester

The best way to generate added speed without sacrificing your unmuscled armswing is to hold the ball higher while in your address position.

The Last Word

In all sports it's human nature to want to do the spectacular. Football place kickers love to boom those 50-yard attempts. Go to basketball camp and you'll see kids firing up three-pointers. In bowling, the big hook ball looks great.

But in all sports it is the athlete who is fundamentally sound who usually prevails.

Don't try to do too much with the bowling ball. Today's equipment is extremely sophisticated. Let the ball do all of the work. After all, that's why you paid so much money for it in the first place!

It is possible to become overly concerned with executing a good shot. If you start thinking of a million and one things you must do with each delivery, chances are you'll be lucky not to drop the ball on your toe! There are many aspects of your shot that will come naturally if all of the preceding motions, such as your release, are correct.

Almost every player worth his salt knows that his thumb exits from the ball before the fingers do. This enables you to get "lift" for added hooking and striking power. It would be silly—not to mention futile—to concentrate on getting your thumb out of the ball first. By executing the fundamentals of a good delivery this will naturally occur.

The key lies at the start. A good address position and a solid pushaway that is coordinated with your footwork will get you well on the road toward success. Conversely, a poor stance and/or pushaway will put you behind the eight ball.

You should practice enough to get to where you can bowl without thinking about your physical game. In most cases the accomplished player steps to the line with but one primary area of concentration: hitting his or her target.

When you are able to consistently perform a smooth and solid delivery the ball will do the rest. Power is a natural derivative of being fundamentally sound. By marrying proper timing with a strong release you will be well on your way toward becoming a vastly improved bowler.

3
SHOOTING SPARES AND SPLITS

by Dave Ferraro

I can't blame most amateurs, even the better ones, for thinking that the key to successful bowling lies in the number of strikes one rolls. In today's age of urethane in which many ultrapowerful players are thriving on tour, the big hook ball must seem very glamorous.

In my world, where one must usually average at least 225 over 42 games to earn a decent weekly paycheck, strikes *are* essential to survival. But for the 150–185 average player, merely filling an extra frame or two per game is the easiest road to improvement. It's not uncommon to find talented amateurs today who would rather need a tenth frame triple to win a match than have to convert a 10 pin. What should be a simple task leaves them virtually trembling with fear.

Spare shooting needn't be a traumatic experience. By applying some basic principles and combining them with a bit of practice you *should* be able to consistently cover your conversion attempts.

Rule number one is that accuracy, not power, is the vital ingredient when covering all spares not involving double wood. I'm amazed how many players try to get 22 revolutions on their ball when shooting at a single pin. You don't need power to knock over a piece of wood weighing less than four pounds. You do need to hit your target.

On this type of conversion, you'll find that while all pros have varying styles, virtually every one of the premiere spare shooters throws his shots directly at the pin(s). There are two good reasons for that.

First, the less one hooks the ball the easier it is to be accurate. It stands to reason that the athlete in any sport who is able to increase his margin for error stands a far greater chance of being consistently successful.

The second factor has to do with lane conditions. As you know, oil deters hook while a dry lane promotes it. For cross-lane spares you will be rolling the ball over a segment of the alley that you do not use for your strike shots. It's very hard to predict if the oil pattern is the same from gutter to gutter or whether, for example, there is an oil buildup in the center of the lane.

The straighter your shot, the less importance is rendered to making a correct "guesstimate." I've seen more than one pro (who should know better) blow a title because he hooked his ball when attempting a single-pin leave. If you roll the ball directly at your target you won't be subjected to the whims of oil patterns that can be as fickle as a Hollywood star.

It's not unusual for PBA Tour newcomers to use big hook balls for all of their shots. More than one of them has taken his lumps on our circuit before going back home to work on his spare shooting. The players who have learned to cover far fewer boards are the athletes who are making a good living year after year.

Even the crankers like Amleto Monacelli and Mark Baker cover fewer boards on their second shot than on their strike balls. In fact, Amleto's steady improvement is owed primarily to his increased ability to convert spares since he has learned to shoot at them more directly.

If you do attend a PBA event, notice how Mark Roth and Joe Berardi shoot their spares. While few of us—myself included—could approach their ball speed, the principle of how they have gone about becoming the best modern-day spare shooters is worth noting. Brian Voss is another player worth emulating. All three roll hard and straight at their spares.

Equally important is that all your motions should be directed right at your target. As basic as that sounds, most bowlers do not do that. Believe it or not, many pros walk toward the left to throw the ball to their right. Before releasing the ball they must get their hips out of the way and their shoulders open to do that successfully. To me, all of those excess motions don't make any sense.

Always be square to your target. Walk toward the pin(s).

It's been my experience that the majority of bowling books and coaches will instruct players to move three boards here and five boards there for various shots. In my opinion, there are no hard-and-fast rules. The only way to find what line works best for you on a specific type of spare is through trial and error.

A player with a natural hook—even one that he's managed to tone down significantly—should not be standing in the same spot for a 10 pin as should a bowler who can naturally roll his ball straight.

There is a school of thought that disagrees with my trial-and-error targeting philosophy. Another option is to always use the third arrow as your target and adjust your feet according to the specific spare.

The key, I feel, is to experiment and do what works best for you. Whether you convert or miss the shot, be certain to make a mental note of where your ball ended up, where you stood on the approach, what you used as a target (and if you hit that target), and whether you rolled the ball correctly.

Only through post-shot analysis can you make modest adjustments on your following attempts. For example, if you miss a spare by two boards to the right, you know to keep the same target and move your feet a board (or two) in the direction that you missed (i.e., the right).

If you don't think, you won't learn. When watching league competition at our bowling center I often see players make a spare on their first attempt and then line up in a completely different position the next time they're faced with the same shot. That tells me they had no idea where they stood or how to aim.

In all phases of bowling, there are no hard-and-fast rules. Unorthodox players can, and have, enjoyed outstanding careers. But all successful bowlers share one common trait: they are constantly thinking. You've probably heard it said hundreds of times by pros that the mental game is what often separates the star from the also-ran. That holds true for amateurs, as well. The better your analytical ability and your concentration, the better you will be able to get the most out of your physical talents.

Unless you can throw the ball as straight as an arrow, you must pay at least some attention to oil patterns. The majority of bowling houses have an oil buildup in the middle of each lane. When that's the case, simply adjusting for a left-sided spare off of your strike line is dangerous.

For example, you've left the 2 pin. Since it's exactly five boards to the left of the headpin, one might assume you would cover it by moving your feet and your target five boards to the left. That sounds logical. However, if the middle boards have more oil than their outer counterparts, your shot will not turn over an inch, resulting in your ball rolling past the right side of the pin.

Few lanes are oiled evenly from gutter to gutter. What separates bowlers from golfers is that we can't see our hazards. The golfer can spot a sand trap or a pond. Our danger areas are, for the most part, invisible. Yes, there are clues one can look for to determine oil patterns. However, they're subtle and it's hard to get a precise read.

For virtually all non-double-wood spares, draw an invisible line from the pin through where you are holding the ball during your address. Where that line intersects at the arrows is your target. If you have a slight hook, move your target a few boards to the right of our imaginary line to compensate (if you are left-handed move your target to the left).

Since it's easier to hit an arrow than a board between them, move your feet a bit to either side if necessary to have an arrow as your target.

Having done that, step directly at that arrow. Employ your straight armswing. Follow through by "throwing" your hand at the target.

There are some spares that call for the same release as when you're shooting at a full rack. That goes for any situation where power is necessary to carry out a double-wood cover (i.e, any leave in which the headpin is not standing that involves at least both the 2 and 8 pins or the 3 and 9 pins).

Sufficient ball revolutions are required so that your ball won't deflect when hitting the right side of the front pin (or, for lefties, the left side of the forward stick).

Having said that, accuracy is still vital so that a looping hook remains a detriment. The ideal situation is to be a Walter Ray Williams who combines a straight shot with more than enough "juice" by using forward roll. He augments his talent by switching to a harder-shell ball for many of his spare attempts (see Chapter 6). While Walter's skill level is well beyond duplication for the typical league participant, there are spare-shooting techniques of the pros that are worth practicing.

There are several steps you can take to roll a ball more directly. First, do not cup your wrist. By keeping your wrist in a natural position you will lessen the hook. To really "kill" your shot, bend your wrist backward. Upon releasing the ball, point your thumb toward the floor as it is farther forward than your fingers. Simply pretend your ball is the handle of a suitcase. Turn that suitcase clockwise and grab it accordingly.

Obviously, the faster a ball travels, the less it hooks. You want to add velocity *without* sacrificing accuracy. Never throw the ball so fast that you are off balance at the line.

To gain speed, accelerate your armswing after the zenith of your backswing. Another possibility is to hold the ball higher during your address. That will lengthen your swing.

The longer the armswing, the more gravity works in your favor as the ball moves downward and forward during your last step. Remember, you will increase your conversion percentage in proportion to the amount that you decrease your hook.

There are many common spares that you must master if you are to progress to the next plateau. In each case, I have listed the southpaw equivalent in parentheses.

The 10 pin (7 pin)   When my coauthor began his great pro career this shot was his nemesis. The 7 pin is the same for Mike as the 10 pin to a right-handed player. Mike's inability to convert it cost him the championship game of the 1982 AMF Grand Prix in Paris when, as the top seed, he missed it twice. Mike worked hard on this aspect of his game. He no longer crosses nearly as many boards on single-pin leaves and, as a result, has become one of the PBA Tour's premiere spare shooters.

For a player like me who doesn't normally hook the ball a lot, the 10 pin is the *only* one that isn't natural to my game on which I must "kill" my release (Mike does the same on his 7 pin conversions *and* when shooting at the 4 pin). On all other non-double-wood spares, I roll the ball in a manner that comes most naturally to me.

On the 10 pin, I make a conscious effort to "kill" my shot by throwing it harder and/or breaking my wrist backward. Only if the lanes are extremely dry do I find it necessary to do both. Otherwise, either adding speed or subtracting from my release will get the job done.

The way that most pros convert the 10 is to stand on the far left side of the approach during their address. They walk directly at the pin and roll the ball over the third arrow. If you are unable to completely "kill" your hook, perhaps you should move your target to the right (as far as between the first and second arrow isn't unusual for a cranker).

Always aim cross-lane. How far you stand to the left is up to you, but you should certainly be to the left of the center dot on your release. The greater your angle, the less the gutter becomes a nemesis.

When attempting to convert a 10 pin, stand on the far left side of the approach and use the third arrow (from the right) as your target.

Speaking of that great blue channel, the best policy is to forget it's there. Like a quarterback who must learn to ignore the opposition's pass rush, you will never become successful if you permit yourself to become preoccupied or intimidated.

Likewise, do not be concerned with the wall when shooting on lane one. If you walk toward your target, the wall should not be a physical factor (whether it's a psychological factor is up to you). The same holds true when bowling in an old center where the ball return apparatus extends to the foul line.

Mark Roth won the King Louie Open three times (1975, 1978, and 1979) in Kansas City in a house in which an extended ball return machine apparatus reached the foul line. Mark would kick it on virtually every shot after he released the ball. He understood that because the contact occurred after the release it wouldn't affect his shot unless he allowed himself to become distracted by it.

That level of concentration is one reason why Mark ranks as one of the greatest players in the history of the sport.

The 7 pin (10 pin)   When rolling the ball from right to left a mild hook will work in your favor. The biggest danger is pulling your shot and having it sink into the left channel. The more you hook the ball, the more important it becomes to aim for the inside (right) half of the 7 pin.

I strongly urge you not to swing the ball out (in other words, don't aim for a lower-numbered board from your release point). Players who make that mistake run the risk of being victimized when encountering unanticipated oil.

The 2 pin (3 pin)   By standing to the right and aiming for the near (right) side of the 2 pin I have enjoyed great success. I use as little hook as possible. However, neither am I overly preoccupied with killing my shot to the point that I would sacrifice the comfortable feeling of a natural delivery.

The chances are that players who don't cover a tremendous number of boards on their first ball can successfully shoot this spare off of their strike line. To do so, retain the same target while moving your feet about three boards to the right.

The bigger your hook, the less of an accurate "read" you can get from adjusting off of your strike lane. That's why you'll have done yourself a great service by learning how to shoot spares the hard-and-straight way. When doing so, move your feet to the right so that the third arrow intersects that imaginary line from your ball to the pin.

Keep in mind that the danger lies in that whenever one crosses over the center of the lane there is the issue of how much oil exists. The more direct you roll the ball, the less you need to worry about unpredictable lane patterns.

I suspect that one could oil 20 lanes 20 different ways

Good spare shooters not only aim cross-lane, but they also keep their bodies square to the target.

and a player like Joe Berardi would still convert each one of his single-pin spares. Because Joe is such a master of rolling the ball straight, the distribution of conditioner on the lane is no longer a factor for him.

Some bowlers shoot the 2 pin from left to right. They stand just inside the left gutter and aim the ball over the sixth arrow (which is the second arrow in from the left).

I suppose that someone who rolls the ball perfectly straight can use this method successfully. Having said that, there aren't many players who roll a ball more directly than I do, and I find this method isn't satisfactory for my game. The reason, again, is the issue of lane conditioner. I have no idea what is on the opposite side of the lane and little desire to discover it the hard way.

Of course, I'm referring to tour conditions. When I tried this method I often found that the head area of the left half of the alley was far drier than the right. As soon as the shot left my hand it began to hook. I won't attempt to describe that helpless, sinking feeling one gets in the pit of the stomach when that occurs. I'm sure that's one part of the game that bowlers know all too well.

The "bucket" (2-4-5-8/3-5-6-9)   Few pin combinations are as difficult as this one. If you hit too squarely on your target pin (the 2 pin for a righty and the 3 pin for the lefty) you will chop it and leave the 5 pin standing. If you are light and/or don't have enough power on your shot, the ball will deflect and leave the back pin.

Making matters more difficult is that the ball must cross to the opposite side of the lane, meaning it will travel over the most unpredictable part of the alley. To top everything off, your confidence probably isn't soaring since you have just made a bad shot that has resulted in your leaving the bucket in the first place.

The first step is to determine what went wrong on your

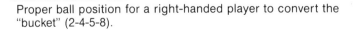

Proper ball position for a right-handed player to convert the "bucket" (2-4-5-8).

Photo by Dan Chidester

strike ball. If your execution was at fault, a simple move of your feet of three to five boards to the right should do the trick (depending on how much you hook your shots).

However, if you felt you made a good shot *and* hit your target, it's possible that the lane has heavy oil. Check the surface of your ball to see if the track area has more conditioner on it than it would under normal circumstances. If that's the case, you may want to move an extra board or two to the right with your feet.

Some players like to move both their feet and their target to the right to get a better entry angle. They are then free to roll the ball a bit more firmly to guard against the chop since this wide angle helps to minimize the deflection danger of leaving the back pin.

By knowing your game you will be able to understand whether the deflection or the chop is your number one enemy. Straighter shooters worry more about the former while power players tend to fear the latter. The big hooker can opt to add ball speed as a precaution while the conventional bowler does just the opposite.

The key is to learn through experimentation what works best for you. There are times when Mike rolls a relatively straight ball at the bucket. That's an approach some pros utilize when the distribution of conditioner is so unpredictable that "reading" the lane is virtually impossible.

The 2-4-5 (3-5-6)   This is the bucket without the back pin. Your only concern becomes chopping the lowest-numbered pin off of the 5 pin. Because of that, rolling the ball straight takes on an even greater premium. If that comes naturally to you, then you may wish to move to the opposite side of the lane. Stand near the far gutter and play the ball over (about) the fifth or sixth arrow. Through trial and error, you will find what works best for your game. Do not try this, however, if you are aware that the other side of the lane is excessively dry or if you have a tendency to pull your shots.

The 2-8 (3-9)   This is similar to the bucket except that now the chop possibility is eliminated. You must hit this either on the middle or the near side of the front pin (i.e., on the right of the 2 pin for a right-handed player and on the left of the 3 pin for a southpaw).

Moving to the right by three or four boards while playing your strike ball is the common adjustment. The less power you generate on your shots, the greater the danger of a deflection. To counter that, decrease your ball speed (by holding the ball lower at the address point and slowing all of your movements during your approach). Also, give yourself a better angle by moving your feet and target to the right.

The 3-9, 3-6-9, 3-6-9-10 (2-8, 2-4-8, 2-4-7-8)   This is a tough assignment. You can neither get a good angle nor use a powerful hook to avoid the deflection. With the combinations involving three or four pins, the possibility of a chop is added. To make matters worse, the far outside of the lane is another unpredictable section.

What to do? Move to the right. A good starting point when experimenting is in the neighborhood of the fourth to the eighth board. The first arrow is a good target.

The picket fence (1-2-4-7/1-3-6-10)   Once again, your strike shot has come up light. Unlike the bucket, there is no backstick. In fact, if your ball deflects it will add to your effectiveness.

If you feel confident with your straight ball, aim directly at the Brooklyn side of the headpin. Use roughly the same line you would to shoot a 2 pin. The big hook player is again advised to cut down on the curvature of his shot, lest his ball hook right past the headpin.

The washout (1-2-10, 1-2-4-10/1-3-7, 1-3-6-7)   You want to hit the Brooklyn side of the headpin so that it slides across the lane and into the corner pin.

I use my strike line and move my feet two to three boards to the right. You want your ball to end up in roughly the same place as it reaches the pin deck as when you're converting the bucket.

To make the washout the ball must hit the far Brooklyn side of the headpin.

An Alternative Strategy

What I have described is the personal method I use for covering my spares. While I believe it's the easiest and most effective approach for the majority of players, there are alternatives.

Mike, who is one of the Tour's most accurate performers, opts to shoot his spares off of his strike line. Using the same target on the lane as he had on his first ball, he moves his feet according to what remains.

For example, if faced with a 3 pin he moves three boards to his left. For a right-handed player, the equivalent adjustment is to move your feet three boards to the right for a 2 pin. The 6 pin (lefty) or 4 pin (righty) calls for a move of a half dozen boards. The 10 pin (lefty) or 7 pin (righty) involves a nine-board move.

The baby split (3-10/2-7)   Although this appears a lot tougher than converting a single-pin leave, it isn't that difficult. Roll the ball with as few revs (revolutions) as possible. By hitting the near side of the front pin, your ball will deflect into the corner stick. There is plenty of room to fit your ball, and the straighter you throw it, the greater your margin for error. Only with an ultrapowerful player is there a danger of the ball not deflecting when it hits the right side of the 3 pin (or, for lefties, the left side of the 2 pin).

A cross-lane angle works best. Using the way you shoot your 10-pin conversions as a guide, move your feet three boards to the right while maintaining the same target.

Another alternative is to shoot hard and straight from the far left side of the approach.

Photo by Dan Chidester

The correct way to shoot the baby split sees the ball covering both pins.

The 3-6-10 (2-4-7)   This is basically the same shot as the baby split, although your margin of error is increased. If you go Brooklyn on the baby split, the front pin often flies around or in front of the corner pin. Do the same on this leave and you'll make it the majority of the time.

Nevertheless, your best bet remains to aim for the near side of the front stick. As such, use the same technique as you do for the baby split.

The 9-10 split (7-8)   I suggest moving a board or two to the right of where you stand for your 10-pin shots. Your ball can fit precisely between the two pins but you'll need great accuracy to make this split. Once again, trial and error will tell you what angle works best for your game.

The 4-5 split (5-6)   The angle is roughly the same as the bucket. Move from three to four boards to the right on the approach of your starting point on your strike shot while retaining the same target.

The backup option for straight shooters is to roll the ball down the left side of the lane so that it fits exactly between the two pins. For the record, I prefer the former option.

The 5-7 split (5-10)   The movement I make is to place my feet two boards to the left of my strike ball while keeping the same target on the lane. From there I feel I know what the lane will do.

The 6-7-10 split (4-7-10)   While it is possible to make this shot, the odds are long even for an established pro. Unless a mark is critical to my winning a match, I will make certain that I at least knock down the 6 and 10 pins. I won't give that pin away otherwise.

When "going for broke," you should shoot almost as if you were aiming for the 10 pin. The only difference would be to move your feet one board to the left of where you stand when shooting the 10 pin.

By rolling your shot hard and straight you give yourself a slightly better chance. The faster your ball moves, the greater the chance that your target pin (which is the lowest-numbered stick in this case) can either bounce out of the pit or hit off of the opposite sidewall.

The 4-9 split (6-8)   I think of this as if I were trying to convert the 7 pin. I might move a board or two right of my 7-pin target to increase my angle. It's my hope that I can nick the far left side of the 4 pin and slide it into the 9 pin.

The 5-10 split (5-7)   This isn't a very common leave, but it can occur when your strike ball drifts far to the Brooklyn side of the headpin. Stand where you would for the bucket (i.e., to the right three or four boards with your feet).

The 5-10 split demands pinpoint accuracy.

Photo by Dan Chidester

"Unmakable" Splits

In bowling, as in life, discretion is usually the better part of valor. There are some splits that are virtually impossible to cover.

I've been bowling since 1961 and I have yet to convert the 7-10, the 4-6, the 8-10, the 4-6-7-10, or what's known as the Greek Church (4-6-7-9-10 or 4-6-7-8-10). Of course, if I can bowl another 30 or so years, there's a very good chance I'll make one of them. After all, accidents do happen.

Which doesn't mean these are impossible. In one of the most amazing exhibitions I've ever seen, Jeff Bellinger made four "unmakable" splits in the same block of a tournament a few years back. I'm sure Jeff would be the first to admit that luck played the key role in his streak on that occasion.

I play it conservative when I'm faced with one of these geometric monstrosities. Rather than attempt to roll the dice on a million-to-one bet, I go for the wood. If I'm on a strike, there is a four-pin differential on the score sheet between getting those three sticks of the Greek Church as opposed to going for it and hitting but one pin.

It never fails to amaze me how many players needlessly donate pins in such situations. Hardly a PBA tournament goes by in which a player doesn't miss cashing or qualifying for the top 24 match play segment by one or two pins. I know how I'd feel if falling one pin short cost me thousands of dollars, especially if I'd tossed away wood.

It's the same at the amateur level. In your 35-week winter league season you will bowl 105 games. Chances are that at least a half dozen of those will be decided by the slightest of margins. The team that makes a determined effort to always "get the wood" on unmakable splits will probably pick up at least a few extra wins.

Take a look at your league's standings when this season ends. I'll bet that an extra four points in the win column would move you up a notch or two. Moreover, since most intermediate-level amateurs face about one unmakable split per game, you can improve your average by a few pins simply by doing what's intelligent in these situations.

There are exceptions. If your team is down by a wide margin late in the game or it's the tenth frame and getting a mark is crucial, a bold attempt becomes the smart decision. On shots like the 8-10 and 7-10, your best bet is to roll the ball straight and with as much velocity as you can generate. If you hit a fraction of an inch to the right of exact center on the 10 pin it is possible that the ball and pin will collide again on the back wall. If that happens, the pin might ricochet across the lane and out of the pit.

It's an extreme long shot. As of this writing, in over 30 years of PBA action only Mark Roth has ever converted the 7-10 in the televised title round of a tournament.

4
COMMON
SHORTCOMINGS OF
INTERMEDIATE
BOWLERS
by Mike Aulby

When I watch amateurs bowl, I'm struck by how many of them are held back by one major flaw in their game. To have become an intermediate-level player you had to have done a lot of things right. Often, however, a major shortcoming can negate several of your hard-earned assets.

To improve you probably need to upgrade some aspects of your delivery. Of even greater import, you must also identify and eliminate a flaw or flaws which hinder your progress.

A common contemporary trap involves trying to do too much with each shot. The reason you've paid over $100 for a urethane ball is it's capable of doing almost everything short of cooking hot dogs at the snack bar. It will do 95 percent of the work for you, if you only let it.

Do not overturn the ball and throw it too hard. Don't put too much body into your shots. Instead, employ a fluid, even motion throughout your delivery. Be relaxed. Let your ball do all the work. After all, a ball will never get tired!

It is glamorous to have an explosive strike shot like Amleto Monacelli or John Gant. The only trouble is that the style they've developed is what works best for them. Do not emulate a player just because his power is awesome.

Instead, remember that one common key to success in any athletic endeavor is to play within your own limitations. That's easier said than done.

I must admit that there have been times in my career when I would observe Steve Cook or John Gant in action. Without realizing it, I would begin to turn the ball more. That subconscious decision did not serve me well. I suspect that Steve and John wouldn't thrive if they copied my slower ball speed.

Play your own game. If a big hook is natural to you, refine it and exploit it to its fullest potential. If you are a stroker, pride yourself on accuracy. Always work to maximize your natural strengths.

Be Headstrong

Another prevalent flaw that is easily correctable is that a great number of players in this category do not keep their heads steady throughout their entire delivery.

Top-level players keep their eyes riveted on their target at all times during their delivery.

Photo by Dan Chidester

If you observe professional bowlers, you'll note that they all have their eyes fixed on their target throughout their delivery. The head does not move either up and down or side to side.

That's an important part of any athletic movement in which an accurate throw or shot is needed. Boxers should bob and weave. The rest of us—except for Fernando Valenzuela—must keep our heads stationary.

That's one reason you should have a target on the lane that's no closer than the arrows. Players who spot at the foul line will have to lower their chin as they move forward. The less steady your head, the less likely you are to produce a good and accurate shot.

There are two main reasons why players fall short in this regard. Number one is that they are moving at an excessive rate of speed during their delivery. The second possibility is that they are so concerned with generating maximum power that their motions are herky-jerky rather than smooth.

Do not be overanxious to see where your shot is going after it leaves your hand. Allowing your head to "pop up" too soon detracts from executing a smooth delivery. That could cause you to hit your release on the upswing. Watch your target until you see the ball roll by it. Doing so will help you achieve a good knee bend and extension on your follow-through.

Leave the Fast Feet to Track Stars

Fast feet are the undoing of many players whose games are otherwise solid. Consistent timing is a prerequisite for a consistent release. Make certain that your pushaway and initial step (or, if you are a five-step player, your second stride) are coordinated. If you don't start right, it's impossible to finish right.

Be careful to avoid the fast pushaway. Many bowlers prematurely drop the ball downward. As a result, the ball is by their side far too soon. That leads to timing difficulties at the release point.

Remember to hand the ball to an imaginary "invisible man." Let gravity pull the ball downward and backward.

Stay Square

Another common error among intermediate-level players is a failure to have their entire body parallel to the foul line at the point of release. It's far easier for a stroker to be "square" than it is for a cranker since the latter tends to open up his shoulders during the backswing. The more you turn your upper body, the less chance you have of being in the desired position when the ball leaves your hand.

Even for the power players of the PBA Tour who roll upwards of one hundred games per week, it's hard to have consistently square shoulders on every shot when opening up significantly during the backswing.

If the pros have problems doing that, imagine how tough it will be for you who aren't able to practice nearly as much. That's why I advise amateurs to keep their motions as simple as possible. The more basic your game, the easier it will be for you to duplicate good shots and eliminate bad ones.

Other Common Errors to Avoid

There are very few accomplished bowlers who don't feature a far better-than-average armswing. Muscles are for Hulk Hogan and Rambo, not bowlers. Mind you, there's nothing wrong with having a good physique; it's just that you should give those biceps the night off when you go bowling.

You can practice that by just swinging the ball from your shoulder without having your arm direct the ball whatsoever. Have it swing back and forth in a straight line. What you feel when doing that is exactly what you should feel when bowling.

It all starts with the proper address position, as outlined on pages 19–22. It continues with a good pushaway in which the ball is "handed" forward on a line even with your bowling shoulder as shown in the accompanying photograph.

Keep the wrist position locked and your elbow straight. Doing both helps your shoulder act as a pendulum as the weight of the ball swings your hand (and NOT the other way around!). Really work in practice on not "helping" your shot by engaging your arm's muscles. That's a far more difficult

Here's an excellent pushaway. Notice how the ball is handed directly forward and is in line with the player's shoulder to allow for a straight armswing.

Photos by Dan Chidester

Do not muscle your swing. A bent elbow is a sign of trouble.

proposition than it sounds, but your ability to master the unmuscled swing could help you reach your next bowling plateau.

Never cut your shot off. A good follow-through is important. Reach out toward your target and then your hand travels upward. Far too many players fail to reach out toward their target. Doing so will help you get more lift on your shot, which will yield a stronger finish. You'll also be more accurate if your follow-through is up to par.

There are bowlers who have averaged in excess of 150 while using a backup ball. While some players, including many women, can and do throw the "reverse curve" quite well, it's a technique that will only get you so far. You need to learn to roll a hook ball if you are serious about becoming the best player that your potential will allow.

There are several areas in which the backup proponent faces handicaps. It's virtually impossible to cover a lot of boards, so power is difficult to achieve. Moreover, to release such a shot requires an inside-out armswing and the use of your arm's muscles, neither of which is desirable.

To compensate, overcompensate. Work at spinning the ball by coming around it. For a left-handed player that means a clockwise release, while righties rotate their bowling hand in a counterclockwise motion.

This is one of those cases when you must be willing to take the proverbial one step backward before you are able to take two steps forward. Yes, at first your scores will probably decrease. Do not become discouraged. Keep in mind that long-term improvement is far more significant than short-term results.

Never underestimate the importance of a strong mental game   While bowling is a physical activity, it's also a test of your knowledge. I guarantee you that if you took the top 100 pros all but a handful can strike at will when faced with a soft condition. Even that number might be conservative.

What separates champions from rabbits is how quickly they make the proper adjustments in hand releases, ball speed, equipment, and lines.

Learning from the Pros

To become a top-flight PBA performer, an athlete needs to possess a wide range of abilities. While being a by-the-book player is far less important in bowling than in any other sport that comes to mind, the great players all have certain common traits.

No matter how unorthodox a bowler may look during his delivery, the good ones all share these traits:

▶Shoulders and hips are square to the target during the release.

▶The hand comes through the ball at the point of release so that the ball goes onto the lane, not into it or upward.

▶Timing—whether by the book, early, or late—is consistent from shot to shot. And consistent timing can only occur when the pushaway and footwork are consistent.

▶Good balance and leverage are achieved at the foul line.

▶Most spare leaves are covered with a direct line by throwing the ball hard and straight.

If you know what to look for, you can learn a lot by observing the top pros in action. The next time you attend a PBA tournament, follow one player around for an entire block. Notice the subtle changes he makes when changing pairs. Observe how he gets to the line virtually the same way on every shot.

If you can't watch us live, use your VCR as a coaching tool. Most units have slow-motion capabilities so you can truly dissect aspects of each player's game.

All of us have strengths and weaknesses. Here, in my opinion, are some of the strong suits of PBA stars that you would do well to emulate.

Photos by Frank Valeri

To obtain a powerful release combined with consistent accuracy you must have good balance throughout.

Overall: Marshall Holman and Brian Voss have great all-around games. Marshall is moderately unorthodox in that he's very low to the ground throughout his delivery. That notwithstanding, his fundamentals, like Brian's, are superb. Others worth copying are Joe Berardi and Dave Husted.

Pushaway: Four of the best are David Ozio, Steve Wunderlich, Berardi, and Husted.

Steady Head: Marshall Holman is excellent. Most any pro, however, scores well in this category.

Leverage: Mark Baker is very solid at the foul line and has an excellent release. Like most power players, Mark's sliding foot is planted prior to his release. Only Marshall Holman is able to generate great power by shooting as he is sliding. Others to watch are Steve Cook, Mark Roth, and Amleto Monacelli. When observing Steve and Amleto, notice how they generate so much power while remaining totally under control. Their last step and work at the line are first-rate.

Release: Mark Williams has an excellent release. He can hook a ball from here to China or he can roll it as straight as an arrow. Walter Ray Williams is unique in that he gets nearly a cranker's power out of a stroker's style with his end-over-end roll. Wayne Webb, like Mark, is a master of a wide variety of releases, which allows him to be competitive on virtually any lane condition.

Lofting: Three of the best lofters are Roth, Voss, and Dave Ferraro.

Kneebend: Steve Cook, especially for a big man, is amazingly accomplished. Walter Ray Williams is another star who uses his sliding leg to full advantage to gain added leverage at the line.

Footwork: Take a look at Holman, Cook, and Husted.

Armswing: For a loose armswing that is both straight and unmuscled, look to Ozio. Don Genalo and Mike Durbin have great swings. Tom Baker is strong.

Walter Ray Williams has a straight swing that is very loose throughout. Fluidity in a natural swing to let the ball do the work is the top priority, which is why Holman's game is so great.

Follow-Through: Pete McCordic, who exaggerates his post-shot form, is outstanding. Ozio and Dave Ferraro are also top-notch.

Adjustments: Some of the most intelligent pros are Webb, Cook, and Ozio.

Sizing Up the Pros

Another aspect of learning by observing is to find a pro whose body type is similar to yours. There would be little logic if six-foot, one-inch Isiah Thomas grew up trying to emulate a seven-foot center like Wilt Chamberlain.

So, too, in bowling. Big guys have special problems, as do those of slighter build. That doesn't mean they can't become great players, as proven by two current superstars, Steve Cook (6'7") and Wayne Webb (5'5").

The taller you are, the more difficult it can be to maintain consistent timing. I know Steve feels cramped by an approach that is far too short for someone with strides that are naturally as long as his are. Even when he stands with his heels over the edge of the approach during his address, he still has too little room with which to work.

I wish there were a magical formula for taller players. The only advice I have is to practice longer and harder at the aspects of the game that are most difficult. Aside from timing, the other problem area is getting leverage at the foul line.

The ideal release point sees the ball a few inches from the ankle of your sliding foot and a couple of inches above the lane. For the tall player, that requires an outstanding kneebend. Always guard against the temptation to bend from your waist.

One of the most amazing attributes that Steve possesses is that his kneebend is as good as anyone's on the Tour despite his height handicap.

Taller bowlers should not be discouraged, for you certainly have many fine role models. The proof lies in three men, each of whom stands six-feet, four-inches tall.

Mark Baker is a former high school basketball star who ranks among the PBA's top performers by using a power-oriented style. In contrast, both Gary Dickinson and Frank Ellenberg are stylists who have carved out very successful careers.

The taller you are, the more cramped the approach will seem. If Steve were to execute a shot using footwork that would feel completely natural he would slide well past the foul line. With less room with which to work you won't feel as claustrophobic when using the four-step delivery. To be successful with it you will have to redouble your efforts at having everything coordinated while executing your push-

Although being tall like Steve Cook (6'7") makes bowling more difficult, it need not stop you from becoming an exceptional player.

Photo by Frank Valeri

away so that your timing will be consistent during your release.

You won't see too many of today's pros with a significant weight problem. That's because fitness is important in bowling. Most of today's top players have daily routines that include exercise such as jogging.

It is still possible to succeed without being in ideal shape. But extra weight is a handicap, especially when rolling several games, as fatigue becomes a factor. If you are to maximize your potential you will need to shed that excess.

For the intermediate-level player with a fuller body, I suggest concentrating on your release. Be extra careful to loft the ball out onto the lane and not upward or downward. As best you can, try to get a good kneebend.

For the smaller player, à la Webb or Tony Westlake (5′6″), generating sufficient ball speed is far from easy. Wayne

An excessive knee bend will force you to bend your elbow, which will cause your shot to lose striking power.

Photo by Frank Valeri

is a master at modifying hand releases so that the ball does what he desires.

Amleto Monacelli, Rick Steelsmith, and Pete Weber are all five-feet, seven-inches tall. They each use a very high backswing with the ball lifted well above head heights. That isn't a style that very many players could copy successfully, however. As such, the shorter amateur player would probably do better using Webb as a role model.

For the typical smaller player, there are steps you can take to get more ball speed. Hold the ball higher during your address. On your pushaway, push the ball upward and forward. As with all bowlers, allow gravity to do all of the subsequent work so that you can obtain a pendulum arm-swing that receives no help from your muscles.

Adding steps can increase momentum. Because of that, the five-step approach usually works better than the four-step variety.

Even with that, do not expect to throw the ball as hard as the big guys. The temptation to "help" your shot's speed by using your arm muscles must be avoided. Players who try to do too much find that for every gain in one area there are more setbacks in other areas. Always stay within the limitations of your natural game. You can become very successful without throwing the ball fast.

5
ANALYZING YOUR FLAWS
by Dave Ferraro

As a bowler you are required to wear two hats. You are at the same time the athlete *and* the coach. Whenever you run into problems, only you can devise your own solutions. This is a source of both frustration and satisfaction.

It can be extremely aggravating when things don't go your way and all attempted solutions are not working. On the other hand, overcoming a difficult lane condition through the combination of your wit and skill is immensely rewarding.

What is required, first of all, is a cool head. Getting angry at alleged taps won't get you anywhere. You can rant and rave all you want, but your antics won't convince a single additional pin to fall.

There are many bowlers, including some pros, whose tempers cost them dearly. It's a comfort to their opponents who know that only a few bad breaks are required to have them self-destruct.

Aside from keeping your composure, you will need to understand both bowling principles and your own game. You must be able to decide what is going wrong and institute the appropriate correction.

No matter how badly things are going for you, you can't

afford to quit. Those few extra sticks you can grind out could win your team the game or contribute toward total wood. Even if the contest is lost, you might discover an adjustment that could give you an edge in a future match.

There are two things I never do when things go wrong.

First, I never blame the lane condition. No matter how low the scoring might be, somebody will still emerge the winner. While shooting a 250 is great, the primary objective in bowling is simply to win. To do so you must finish at least one pin ahead of the opposition. You will never see me turning down a 171–170 victory. Hey, a win is a win!

I know this will sound arrogant but the second thing I don't do is think that the problem lies with my game. In the locker room after a block I often hear players saying things like "I bowled terribly tonight." I never think it's me.

If my scores are awful, I assume it's because I couldn't figure out which piece of equipment and/or what line would work best. But I always feel I bowled well.

As a professional my game has reached a certain level whereby I feel I'm able to pretty much duplicate the same stroke shot after shot, game after game, and tournament after tournament. I understand that the occasional participant who rolls a limited number of games a week isn't able to achieve anywhere near the same level of consistency that I should.

There will be times when the difficulty will lie in your physical game. However, you should take a page from my book and never allow yourself to think that you can't overcome your problems. Always work to grind out every pin of each game that you can possibly get.

There are two types of adjustments you can make. Either there is a physical flaw that has crept into your delivery and must be eradicated or you need to change how you are playing the lane. The latter calls for a new line or different equipment.

Playing the Lane Differently

One of the biggest problems people have is not moving

around on the approach. They play the exact same line from one alley to another despite the fact that no two lanes are precisely the same.

It's hard for me to believe my eyes when I see a talented amateur hit the beak on several consecutive shots without any hint of making an adjustment. But it happens, and it happens a lot to players who ought to know better.

Make lane moves/ adjustments only after physically executing a good shot.

Photo by Frank Valeri

Learning from your mistakes is the only way to implement a correction. Watch your ball with trained eyes on every shot. Both the pin reaction and the way your shot rolls will provide vital information if you are sufficiently astute in your observations.

The first rule of changing lines or equipment is that you only do so after you have physically executed a good delivery. There is no point in trying to read a shot that hasn't been rolled properly.

When your body has done what your mind wished it to do, you can make an educated guess as to how to play the lane better. It's at the point when you must decide what change is most appropriate.

There are two basic problem areas. Perhaps you are missing the pocket altogether. When that's the case, make a move on the approach in the direction that you are missing while maintaining the same target on the lane. In other words, if your ball is going too far to the right you should move your feet to the right. If you are missing left, move to the left.

To put it another way, let's say you are a right-handed bowler who is going Brooklyn and or/is consistently high on your strike attempts. A simple move to the left should rectify your problem. On the other hand, if your shots aren't getting up to the pocket, move your feet to the right. Move the opposite way if you are a southpaw.

The other possibility is that you are hitting the pocket but aren't carrying. When that occurs, I recommend an adjustment only when you are faced with a succession of "weak" leaves.

A "weak" or "deflection" leave results when your shot lacks adequate hitting power at the point of impact. Ideally, your ball will drive into the pocket and power through the rack. It will send the 5 pin into the 8 pin as it then takes out the 9 pin (vice versa for lefties).

A good shot sets off a chain reaction. The ball, having driven through the headpin, hits the side of the 3 pin which, in turn, eliminates the 6 and 10 pins. For southpaws, it is the 2 pin which takes care of the 4 and 7 pins.

On a "weak" hit, your ball will be deflected by the headpin to the side (to the right for right-handed players and to the left for left-handed bowlers).

Among the leaves you will see if you are right-handed are the 5 pin, the "soft" 10 pin, the 5-7, and the 8-10. Left-handed bowlers will encounter the 5 pin, the "soft" 7 pin, the 5-10, and the 7-9.

What do I mean by the "soft" 10 pin? There are two categories of corner pin leaves. The "ringing" 10 pin occurs when the 6 pin flies up and around the 10. For the southpaw, the "ringing" 7 pin results when the 4 pin flies up and over it.

In contrast, the lower-numbered pin is pushed weakly into the gutter on the "soft" leave. While the end result is identical, the reason for the resulting spare attempt is different.

On the "ringing" variety you made a pretty decent shot. I wouldn't make an adjustment for this leave other than, perhaps, purchasing a new rabbit's foot. Just consider it an occupational hazard that comes with the territory.

Only if you are faced with a succession of ringing 10s should you contemplate an adjustment. When that's the case, simply move four to six inches farther away or closer to the foul line during your starting position.

Feel free to move forward if you don't think you are likely to foul by using less of the approach. If fouling is a concern, your starting position can be farther back. Either way, you will have altered your ball's breakpoint ever so slightly, which should make the difference.

The "weak" hit calls for a change. The easiest alteration is to move your feet from half a board to an entire board to the right (to the left for a left-handed player). That *should* solve the problem.

Most times it will do the trick. There will be times, however, when you will continue to hit the pocket without getting results. That's when you might consider an equipment change.

Remember, only your eyes can tell you if your ball is performing the desired skid-roll-hook pattern.

By watching your ball you can accurately diagnose your problem. Is the ball rolling out? In other words, is it hooking prematurely so that it has lost much of its hook and hitting power by the time it reaches the pins? Conversely, your ball might not be getting into a roll soon enough.

When the problem is rollout, the physical solution is to loft your shot. Your alternative is to make an equipment change by going to a ball that doesn't hook as much. As Mike described in Chapter 2, you need to get your shot out onto the lane. Concentrate on hitting through the ball on your release.

A shot that skids too far down the lane will not finish at

Photo by Dan Chidester

When done correctly, imparting loft helps to avoid rollout.

the back end. To decrease the skid, roll your ball smoothly over the foul line. A deep bend of the knee of your sliding leg is essential to proper execution. An alternative is to keep the same release while cupping your wrist more.

Having stated that many amateurs do not make any adjustments when things go wrong, it should be mentioned that there are players who go to the opposite extreme. They make major changes in the line they're playing or the equipment they're using after their first tap. Premature changes and overreacting are just as bad as not making any adjustment.

When to Implement a Change

Yes, bowling's objective is to knock down as many pins as possible. Remember, though, that since you are competing toppling one more pin than the opposition is all you really need.

Because of that, you should observe how everyone else is bowling. If your teammates and opponents are struggling, it could be that a difficult condition is the main culprit.

When that's the case, you know that simply filling as many frames as possible is the key to victory. If you aren't carrying but you are hitting the pocket, a big adjustment is not advisable.

Instead, perhaps a move of as little as a half board in one direction or the other could be the difference between striking and leaving a weak 10 pin or that pesky 4 pin. By watching your ball intently after it's released you should be able to reach the proper conclusion as to what changes, if any, are required.

PBA titles have been won by pros using a grindout strategy. Amleto Monacelli claimed the 1988 Showboat Invitational title and the $33,000 champion's purse by correctly realizing and adjusting to his perception that scoring would be very low.

Seeded third entering the television finals, he watched as Gip Lentine edged Walter Ray Williams, 190–189, in the opening match. After seven frames of trying every adjustment he could imagine in his duel with Lentine, Monacelli had suffered two opens and did not have a strike to his name. With a score of 84 in the sixth frame, he was on pace for a sub-150 game.

Luckily for Amleto, Lentine was also struggling. As he stood on the approach in the eighth frame, Monacelli trailed by but five pins. Realizing that the championship pair was virtually unplayable, Monacelli decided to eliminate almost all of his normally big hook shot. He fired every successive strike shot hard and straight at the pocket.

Although Amleto knew he wouldn't strike a lot using that technique, he correctly surmised that he also wouldn't be faced with a succession of splits and washouts.

He was right.

Staying clean the rest of the way, Monacelli knocked off Mark Williams and Mark Roth after having disposed of Lentine. Although Amleto had but one double entering the tenth frame of the semifinal match with Williams, he had already clinched the win when his opponent opened twice.

Similarly, Monacelli beat Roth in the title game. Roth started strong, filling the first seven frames while doubling in the fifth. Amleto had a slight lead, thanks to strikes in frames four through six. In the eighth, Roth barely missed covering the 2-10 split. Amleto filled every frame, which proved the difference in a 215–189 match.

The same strategy would have been a disaster had scoring been high. When everyone else is bowling up a storm, you had better make your move quickly and decisively if you are struggling. Don't be afraid to change lines or equipment.

The Strategy on Playing the Lane Condition Properly

Your main incentive in making adjustments is to find the shot that gives you the greatest margin for error. In every PBA event there are at least a half dozen different angles and as many balls that I could use that would yield strikes if I responded with perfect execution.

The hardest part of reading lanes is ascertaining exactly where to play that will give you the most variation while still letting you hit the pocket. Anyone can produce strike after strike by hitting the exact same board after producing the identical release and ball speed.

If you can do that, YOU should be writing this book. To the best of my knowledge, there has yet to be a bowler who could even dream of approaching such a level of consistency.

Being only human, I won't throw every shot the way that I want to roll it. On the majority of their deliveries, pros commit a few minor errors. The trick is to have found the optimum line and ball so that minor errors are camouflaged.

The expression one hears on the Tour is that a player has "five boards to play with." That means that a person can miss his target by a few boards in either direction and still strike. The power players tend to create more area but they pay a price in greatly decreased accuracy. Strokers are very accurate but lack a sufficient margin of error to produce consistently big scores.

There is a happy medium. Witness the world of the "tweeners." That's a word derived from "in-between" for the players who fall in the middle of the two extremes. These are the guys who consistently excel on a wide variety of lane conditions since they combine good power with good accuracy.

The best pros are the smartest pros. While precious few bowlers have ever possessed the natural ability of a Marshall Holman or a Mark Roth, many athletes with no more than a good level of inbred talent have become great players.

What separates them from the pack are their mental attributes. The pros who finish among the top 10 in yearly earnings several times don't get to that level by accident. They work hard and know what they're doing.

Likewise, you can considerably raise your average without improving your physical game one iota. I could virtually guarantee almost every intermediate-level amateur a 20-pin-

1988 Bowler of the Year Brian Voss possesses a marvelous mental game.

Photo courtesy of the PBA

per-game increase if I could put the brain of a Brian Voss or a Mike Aulby on their shoulders.

One factor to keep in mind is that scores are relevant to lane conditions. Players don't shoot a series of big numbers unless they have significant variation with which to play. On the other hand, if scoring is poor, you might wish to use a more direct line to the pocket to negate the oil's effect.

There is a general rule of thumb you should memorize. The lower the scoring is, the fewer boards you should cross. The easier the condition, the more boards you can cover. Yes, like all rules, this one has its exceptions, but it does apply far more often than not.

Observe your fellow bowlers. If some guy is shooting the lights out it behooves you to note where he's playing. That's especially true if he falls into the same bowling category as you do (cranker, tweener, or stroker).

Thanks to my brother Steve's advice, gleaned by watching a pro whose style is similar to mine, I made the change in my game that's been most responsible for my subsequent success.

The turning point in my career occurred at the 1985 Old Spice Classic, a tournament won by none other than my coauthor, Mike Aulby. Like many young pros, I was more concerned with rolling a "pretty" ball. You know the type of shot to which I'm referring: one that covers about 30 boards with a few hundred revs and sends the pins flying through the roof.

As I entered the final 6-game qualifying block I wasn't even in the top 53 positions which would receive a check. My "pretty" ball wasn't doing a whole lot. A few pairs to the side was Mike Durbin who, unbeknownst to me, was rolling his shots directly at the pocket with astounding success.

Steve came up to me and said, "What in the world are you doing? Aren't you looking at how Mike is playing?" I told him that I was too worried about my own game to notice anyone else's. He told me to just go hard and straight at the pocket.

That's exactly what I did. In six games I went from being

out of the cash to qualifying for match play. I ended up the week in 15th place, $2,200 richer and a whole lot wiser. I immediately decided that four-figure paychecks look a lot prettier than big hook shots that don't knock over enough wood.

The lesson is simple: always play within your abilities and never try to be something that you're not naturally cut out to be. Mark Baker or Amleto Monacelli would probably go broke if they tried to bowl like me. I discovered that I was doing the same when I attempted to emulate them.

Forget about how your ball looks. Leave the style points to the gymnasts. Do what you have to do to knock over the most pins. I've never seen an X that looks bad next to my name on the scoreboard, and I'm sure I never will.

Minor adjustments   Although they're made of wood, pins can talk. When you leave a series of 4 pins (6 pins for a lefty) or several soft 10s (soft 7s), the pins are telling you that it's time to make a move.

When you've left the ringing (solid) 10 pin you have made a good shot. An adjustment isn't called for until it occurs several times. At that point, move up or back approximately a half foot on the approach. The slight difference in pocket entry angle should prove helpful.

While six inches seems like a lot, in most cases your subconscious mind takes over and you conclude your slide very close to your normal distance from the foul line. It's a very minute change. The soft 10 requires a slight and immediate adjustment, *if you have rolled the ball correctly.* Remember, you never move after a physical mistake.

The soft 10 can be a warning signal of a changing lane condition. On short oil it's not unusual to encounter what is known as "carrydown." That occurs when a series of shots literally move the conditioner farther down the lane than it had been initially applied. The result is less finish on the back end.

That has happened to me several times on short oil. The same shot that had produced several consecutive strikes begins to leave soft 10s. When you are using the same line as others on your pair and/or you roll several shots over the same portion of the lane, carrydown is not uncommon.

If you fail to adjust you may pay the price in subsequent frames by leaving a deflection split (such as the 8-10 or 5-7) as the problem worsens.

I suggest moving one board to the right with your feet. Be careful not to move too far lest your next shot go through the nose. If that change isn't enough you can always move another board the following frame on that lane.

It is possible to increase or decrease your hook by adjusting your hand position or ball speed. That's a far more difficult proposition than moving your feet. Only if I have moved right several times and the results stay the same will I consider making one of those physical adjustments.

The 4-pin results when your ball is high. Once again, a slight move is in order. As always, move your feet in the direction to which your shot missed. Since you went high your ball was too far left as it hit the pins, so move your feet about one board to the left while maintaining the same target on the lane.

If you hit the headpin right on the beak, move a couple of boards to the left (the opposite holds true for lefties). Conversely, if you leave a washout move a few boards in that direction (to the right).

Do not, however, move after every single-pin leave. If any back pin except the soft 10 (or, for lefties, soft 7) is standing, you made a fairly good shot. Why mess with success? Do not expect to carry every pocket hit. If the top pros can't do that, neither can you.

Change with the Lanes

The longer the format of your competition, the more likely that you will face a changing lane condition. The same shot that had been working so beautifully suddenly starts charging into the nose or comes up several boards light. Don't panic. You haven't begun making a physical mistake all of a sudden.

What's far more likely is that the lane is doing one of two things. It might be "breaking down" (hooking more) as a succession of shots causes the conditioner to evaporate; thus, the high hits. On the other hand, oil might be carrying down so the back ends are now tighter.

What to do?

I recommend a "two-and-one" adjustment. That's where I move two boards with my feet while altering my target one board in the same direction. As always, move toward where your shot went (if the ball strayed to the left, move your feet and target to the left).

The reason the two-and-one move is so effective is that it allows you to retain the same pocket entry angle as had proven successful before the lane began changing.

Physical Flaws

One of the toughest things for the typical amateur to decide is whether or not a bad shot was caused by a physical mistake.

I know that many players say if they can't feel the ball coming off of their hand they know they have executed a good release. I can also see if I have hit my target. Even if both of those factors are present, it's not necessarily a safe assumption that my body did its job properly.

That's why I like to observe my ball's label. Another good visual tracking device is your ball's finger grips. Either of these two should allow you to notice the amount of revs you are generating. If it varied from your normal roll you know that something was wrong with your delivery (as opposed to the problem being a changing lane condition).

If I can feel the ball on my backswing or during my release, I know that something wasn't right.

I'm sure every player has a different physical key. Getting to know yours is an important step toward becoming able to analyze your match mistakes.

For every miscue, there is a correction.

Dropping the ball   Losing the ball on the downswing is a sure way to sacrifice accuracy and power. The possible causes:

1. Your shoulders are too far forward so you are bent from your waist, not from your knee. This causes you to throw the ball into the lane rather than onto it.

2. Your timing was later than normal.

3. You didn't have a good grip inside the ball and it slipped out of your hand. This could be due to perspiration or a thumb hole that is too large and needs to have some tape inserted.

Throwing the ball upward The other extreme, which is equally undesirable, is to project your shot upward. You again sacrifice power. It's also very difficult to retain accu-

If your shoulders are too far forward you will roll the ball into the lane instead of onto it.

Photo by Dan Chidester

racy unless you can obtain the same distance shot after shot, which is highly unlikely.

The most probable causes:

1. Instead of hitting your release through and out, you have tried to do too much with it. Remember to keep your wrist and hand locked into the same position throughout the entire armswing. Always attempt to keep your ball's loft parallel to the floor.

2. You could have pulled your eyes off your target prematurely. That, in turn, caused your upper body to rise up at the line.

3. Your thumb hole is too tight. Remove a piece of tape.

Missing your target   Minor league baseball is overflowing with pitchers who can throw 90-mile-per-hour fastballs but don't have sufficient control. So, too, with the PBA's regional circuit. There are scores of such players who generate more power than I. Luckily for me, they enjoy limited success because they don't hit their target consistently.

As in golf where it is said of putts, "never up, never in,"

When lofting your shot, do not throw the ball upward.

Photo by Frank Valeri

Staying down during your release is important.

Photo by Dan Chidester

you won't strike if you miss the headpin regardless of how many revs your ball generates.

There are times when you will concentrate on hitting your target yet keep missing to one side or the other. If your shots keep going to the inside of your aiming point you could be:

1. Pulling the ball. Most likely your ball is getting to the point of release too soon. The solution is to put the ball into motion more slowly during your pushaway.

2. You could be pulling up at the foul line. Try to keep your head stationary with your eyes "glued" to your target.

3. Your swing isn't acting as a pendulum. Instead, you are muscling the ball with an outside-to-inside swing. Get that pushaway directly in front of your bowling shoulder and let the ball swing your arm.

On the other hand, you might experience a series of

Rearing up on your shot causes a number of problems.

Photo by Dan Chidester

shots that you miss to the outside. The probable culprits:

1. Dropping your bowling shoulder (the left shoulder for a left-handed player, the right one for a righty).

2. Dropping the ball on the downswing. If that's the case, check to see if you had your weight too far forward. The correction is to be more upright during your delivery so that you will bend at the foul line from your knees and not from your waist.

3. Your swing is moving from inside to outside. Once again, the proper pushaway technique provides the cure.

As you probably noticed, a muscled armswing can cause you to miss in either direction. That's why the combination of a correct pushaway and a pendulum swing in which the ball propels your arm (and NOT vice versa!) is so vital.

If you are able to avoid incorporating your arm's muscles into your swing, all that will be required for a straight motion is a proper pushaway.

A correct (straight) armswing.

Photo by Dan Chidester

This is one of the most prevalent flaws I have noticed that hampers the intermediate-level player. It all starts with having a poor ball position during the address. Remember, place the ball in line with your shoulder and hold it at approximately waist height. Follow that with a proper pushaway, "lock" your wrist/hand into a set position throughout your swing, and let the ball do the rest.

Ball not finishing   If you are hitting your target but your shot goes (skids) far longer than anticipated before hooking, your ball will never get up to the headpin. Should the shot be but a board or two light, there could be carrydown or you might have made a slight mistake. You must decide which is the case.

If you are unsure, do not make an adjustment. Remember, the shot that is slightly light usually won't hurt you nearly as much as a high hit. If you make an adjustment and

Two examples of poor swings with the ball too far to the side (left) and wrapped behind the player's back (right).

the lane hasn't changed, you will go through the nose on your subsequent shot.

However, a miss of several boards that sees the headpin untouched is a sign of a physical mistake. Lanes do not change that dramatically from frame to frame.

You might have thrown your shot too fast. Check your address position to make sure you haven't begun to hold the ball higher than normal. Other possibilities are fast feet and/ or a muscled armswing. Make sure your next pushaway is correct and well timed.

Make certain that you keep that first step slow. It's far easier to alter your initial stride than your subsequent ones. Remember, if you start correctly you should finish correctly.

You could also have lost the ball on your downswing. That makes for a poor release and a shot that lacks power.

Going through the nose when you hit your target might be the result of decreased ball speed. Again, check your address position. If you are holding the ball lower than normal you will have unknowingly shortened your armswing. When you have an unmuscled swing that is controlled by gravity, the shorter swing will cost you ball speed.

Ironically, the opposite could also make your shot "soft." Too much muscle sometimes can impede the arm-swing, also causing your shot to roll more slowly.

Concentrate on being aggressive. Although it involves using a little bit of your arm's muscles, you can work on accelerating through your shot as you begin your down-swing.

If you have a problem of throwing the ball too fast you can make an easy correction. In general, the speed of your armswing corresponds to the pace of your feet. Slowing down that first step should help keep your legs under better control and, with that, your ball at a more desirable (slower) speed.

6
EQUIPMENT
by Dave Ferraro

It's been said that no jockey—no matter how talented—has ever won the Kentucky Derby while riding a mule. In bowling, the same axiom holds true for equipment.

Purchasing a bowling ball used to be as simple as buying a shirt: find one in a nice color that fits and you were in business. Today, however, there is a wide variety of balls made from materials as dissimilar as rubber and polyurethane. Finding the ball or balls that are right for you depends on your game and the oil pattern of the lanes on which you're playing.

It's not unusual for a professional bowler to use a half dozen or more different balls during the course of a tournament. That's because even subtle changes in lane conditions affect ball reaction. That, in turn, alters everything from accuracy to carrying power.

While you, the serious amateur, don't need anywhere near the arsenal of a pro, it is advisable to have at least two to three different types of balls at your disposal.

Likewise, as a contemporary player you have a wide variety of equipment available designed to maximize your

Photo by Dan Chidester

Good pro shops, such as Kingston's Mid City Lanes, carry a wide variety of bowling balls and accessories.

skills. Helpful items range from shoes to wrist supports, from finger grips to bowler's tape, and from urethane balls to rosin bags.

By becoming more knowledgeable about what's on the market you will best select the tools which, when used properly, can increase your scoring by at least 10 pins a game.

One word of caution: bowling equipment is not unlike fashion. When worn on the body of someone in fine shape, some daring styles look fantastic. Put that same outfit on others who aren't quite as slim and it will actually diminish their appearance. Putting a soft-shell urethane monster in the hands of a lousy bowler makes about as much sense as dressing Roseanne Barr in a bikini.

The most sophisticated balls and various other devices are great *once* you have developed your skills. In the hands of novices the same items are counterproductive to maximizing one's potential.

Balls that do the work for the player can be used as shortcuts. Yes, it is possible to "buy a hook." When the lower-average player does so by purchasing a very soft-shelled ball, that bowler will never be forced to learn how to execute the proper hand release required for a powerful shot. Because of that, the player may gain some short-term benefits but he or she will never progress beyond mediocrity.

However, if you have reached the 160-plus plateau, you are probably ready to step up to the world of $50 shoes and $125 bowling balls. If that sounds a bit pricey, it is. Serious players shouldn't be deterred.

Buying two balls for $250 sounds expensive but, given their life expectancy and what they'll do for your game, they're a bargain. For those of us who distribute roughly a half dozen Titleists into the trees and ponds during a typical round of golf, we find that our ball costs per outing are a lot less in bowling than on the links or even when on the tennis courts.

So, too, with accessories. Because you are serious about improving your game, you should carry a wide range of items with you to the lanes. In this segment we'll discuss everything from tape to rosin bags to bowling bags.

Let's start with the most pivotal item of all: your ball.

Bowling Balls

Bowling sure has come a long way from the era of the wooden sphere. As recently as the late 1970s, the state-of-the-art ball was made of plastic. Then came urethane in the early 80s, and bowling hasn't been the same since.

For you, the intermediate and above-level player, urethane is a must. It's vastly superior to its rivals. Because urethane balls hit the pins so much harder, hook more, and track the lane far better, they're worth 10 to 15 sticks per game. Despite its cost, urethane has virtually rendered plastic and rubber as obsolete as the wooden tennis racket.

Each of the six major manufacturers offers several varieties of urethane balls. While some companies are better than others, all urethane balls, like color televisions, have reached a level of excellence.

Each company's line has balls for the three major lane conditions: balls that hook a lot (for oily lanes), medium hookers (for in-between lanes), and relatively straight balls (for dry lanes).

If you are planning on buying but one urethane ball to start with, I suggest opting for the middle-of-the-road variety *unless* your game dictates otherwise. The exception would be if you want to minimize a huge hook (go with the shiny/harder-shell ball) or if you want to greatly increase your hook (pick the dull finish/softest-shell ball you can find).

If you want to have two balls, pick one at either end of the urethane spectrum (a hooker and a nonhooker). This will give you some degree of versatility.

Many pros like to switch balls to cover spares and splits that don't involve double wood. The harder-shell ball (which hooks less) allows you to aim directly at your target. When you throw your shot more straight you lessen the chance of being victimized by an unpredictable oil pattern.

When you move up to urethane you could keep your old rubber or plastic balls for this very purpose. Because they hook even less, they could prove useful on extremely dry lanes when you want to roll the ball straight to convert these types of spares. There have been times when I've used a hard plastic ball for shooting single-pin leaves on the right side of the lane.

Not every pro agrees with this strategy. I know of many players who claim that changing balls robs them of having a consistent "feel" since no two grips are ever exactly alike. In my opinion the value of having a ball that hooks so much less overrides such considerations, but the final decision is up to the individual player.

By the way, should the softer-shell ball hook too much for you to control it, you can decrease the number of boards it covers. Simply shine it in one of those machines that is present at almost all centers.

What the Lustre King unit does is apply wax to the ball's surface. That substance fills in the pores of the track area. It will add early skid to your shot, thus delaying its roll. The wax can add life to your ball. As it wears off the ball will once again hook more.

Photo by Dan Chidester

The Lustre King machine is used to extend ball life.

Don't leave your ball in the machine too long. Start with the lowest cycle of one minute. Then test your ball in action to determine if it needs to be shined some more. Think of this like cooking a steak: once it's overdone, it is ruined. But you can always toss it back on the "grill" if it hasn't been "cooked" enough.

Conversely, you can make the shiny ball hook more by sanding it. Again, it's better to do it too little and try it out before sanding it some more, rather than overdoing it. Remember that American Bowling Congress specifications require you to sand the entire ball, not just the track area.

An alternative to sanding is using a Scotch-Brite pad, which should be available at your local pro shop. This item is a form of steel wool. It's less abrasive than sandpaper. Because of that, the change in your shot's characteristics won't be as drastic. The ball will roll more evenly than when it's sanded. Moreover, a sanded ball has a tendency to overreact (hook a great deal) initially but underreact later on as the effects of the sanding wear off.

If, like most people, you're competing on short oil (where only the first 23 feet after the foul line are covered with lane conditioner with the remaining 37 feet to the pins being dry), a sanded ball is virtually obsolete. Putting a soft-shell, sanded urethane ball on short oil will give you the biggest hook since Kareem Abdul-Jabbar retired.

If you were to have three balls I would suggest one very dull one, another that's glossy, and a middle-of-the-road ball.

The wide variety of urethane balls gives even the slightly better-than-average player far greater versatility than even the best pro enjoyed in the pre-urethane era. If, for example, your ball isn't hooking enough or is leaving a lot of spares on seemingly good pocket hits, go to a softer-shell (duller) ball. If it's hooking way too much, use a harder surface ball.

Do not change balls after bad shots or when you're only missing by tiny margins. In cases like that, modest adjustments in your game are required, as outlined earlier.

When you're "missing by a mile," it's far easier to switch equipment than it is to adjust your hand position on your release or the speed of your shots. That's why good bowlers need *at least* two very different balls at their disposal.

The amateur's all-around arsenal   The more serious and the better you become, the more balls you'll want to carry. Many top amateurs and the majority of pros own equipment produced by several different companies. Doing so allows us to make modest adjustments. I can add as little as a couple of boards of hook by switching to Brand A's soft urethane ball from Brand B's counterpart. I can alter my shot's pocket entry angle while retaining the same amount of hook by using Brand C's most porous ball.

More importantly, such changes may yield a far greater amount of area that you can hit and still strike. Obviously, if you can increase your margin for error, you will enjoy a commensurate rise in the number of shots you carry.

Such seemingly minor adjustments often represent the difference between success and failure both on the pro tour and in top amateur events. The player who recognizes what is required before his opponents do puts himself at a great competitive advantage.

A good rule is to select the softest ball you can use on that condition without the amount of hook becoming a detriment to your accuracy. The reason is that the softer the ball, the less it's likely to deflect when meeting the pins. The improvement in carry can mean 10–20 pins per game.

The proper fit   Why buy a bowling ball from your bowling center's pro shop when you can get one cheaper at the department store down the street?

Would you buy a pair of dress pants from a store that had a lousy tailor? I wouldn't.

You can't release the ball with maximum effectiveness unless it fits properly. If the holes are too big, you will be forced to squeeze your grip so the ball will come off of your hand early. If it's too tight you won't have a smooth exit from the ball, which will hinder accuracy and power. A lousy fit can also lead to a variety of hand and/or wrist injuries.

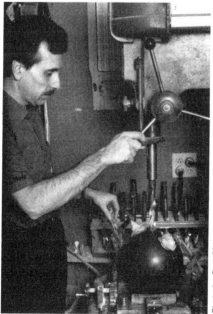

An experienced professional drills thousands of balls a year.

Photo by Dan Chidester

In the opinion of almost all of the top ball drillers with whom I've spoken, the holes fit properly when your fingers and thumb touch one side of the ball while just missing the other. The span—the distance between the thumb and finger holes—must be correct. If all the span isn't right, the ball will not come off of your hand at the proper instant. Even slight changes make for big differences in results.

Your hand size changes from day to day and even during the same day. Your fingers tend to be bigger in the morning than they are later in the day.

Before I drill a ball for one of my customers I always inquire as to whether his or her rings feel loose or tight at the time. This gives me a better read on both the normal and maximum sizes of the fingers and thumbs.

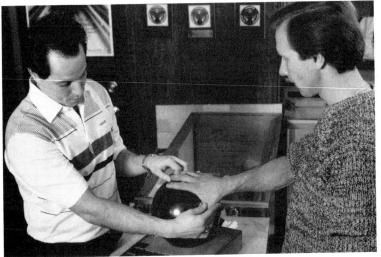

Photo by Dan Chidester

The expertise of the pro shop owner yields a custom fitting that's far superior to one you would normally receive from a sporting goods store.

The ball that you buy must not only fit your hand, it must also fit your game. When new customers enter my pro shop at Mid City Lanes, I make every attempt to watch them bowl. That tells me which type of ball is most likely to best suit their needs. If it's not possible to watch them I will ask several questions concerning how they bowl.

Be wary of someone who tries to sell you a piece of equipment with the claim that it's the "best ball" on the market. What works best for Marshall Holman might be a disaster when in the hand of Walter Ray Williams (and vice versa).

The knowledgeable pro can maximize the effectiveness of your bowling ball by putting in just the right pitches and/or positive or negative weights to best suit your game.

When we refer to a bowler with perfect pitch, we aren't recognizing a new singing sensation. Rather, pitch refers to the angle at which the holes are drilled. Even the slightest variances can be used to increase or decrease the amount of lift on the ball.

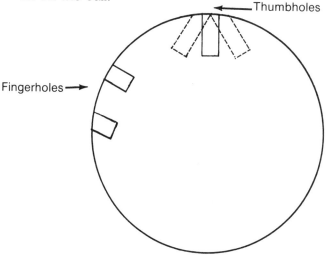

Negative or positive ball pitch can be used to aid your game.

Grips   There are three basic varieties of ball grips: conventional, fingertip, and semifingertip. These refer to how far your middle and ring fingers are meant to enter into your ball.

A *conventional* grip is one in which your two fingers enter the ball up to and including the second knuckle joint. On the *fingertip* grip, your fingers only go into the ball to the first joint. As the name implies, the *semifingertip* is in-between.

Chances are, your first ball was a conventional model. This is best for the neophyte and the developing player as it allows for maximum control.

As you have progressed to become a better-than-average player, you should have graduated to a fingertip grip. This will cause your accuracy to suffer somewhat at first. However, you will get far more revolutions on the ball.

This occurs because your thumb exits earlier on your shot, thus increasing the time when the ball is held only by your fingers. The amount of "lift" you get on your shots—and, with that, revolutions on the ball—should dramatically increase.

My general rule is that once your average tops 150 you are ready for a fingertip grip.

I'm not a big fan of the semifingertip grip. It was popular in my Dad's era. My reason is that with no joint that matches up to the edge of the ball you don't have a barometer by which you can gauge whether your fingers have entered the ball far enough or too deeply. Thus, you rarely grip your ball the same way twice.

A = Fingertip

B = Semi-fingertip

C = Conventional

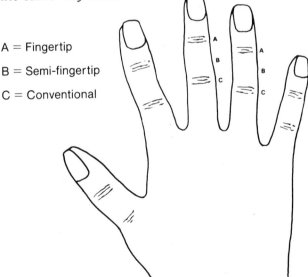

The fingertip grip sees you insert your fingers only up to the first joint. In contrast, the conventional grip goes to the second joint while the semi-fingertip grip lies halfway between the two extremes.

The result is that the player often places his or her fingers either too far or not far enough into the ball with each error, in effect, altering the span. That causes the thumb exit to vary which, in turn, hurts your release.

If you go in too deep the span is increased. That gives you a late release. Not entering far enough makes for a shortened span and an early release.

Finger grip inserts   It is from the lift we get from our fingers during our shot's release that we are able to generate pin-shattering power. It stands to reason that greater leverage will result if you can delay the time frame between when your thumb exits the ball and when you conclude your release with your fingers. That's the entire principle behind using finger grip inserts.

Also on the market are thumb inserts. Their greatest attribute is that they enable you to maintain the same feel when switching from one ball to another. They come in varying hardnesses. Some are ribbed, others are smooth. They can even be used to add pitch.

You can buy the finger grip inserts in materials ranging from urethane to silicon to rubber. The rubber ones stick to your fingers the most and thus provide the latest release for maximum lift. Silicon and urethane are more slippery than rubber so your fingers don't stay in the ball quite as long.

Although the majority of today's professionals use them, finger grip and thumb inserts aren't for everybody. If you have a problem with hanging in the holes during your release these things will make it that much worse. Consult a pro who knows your game to determine what, if anything, is probably best suited to your needs. After some trial and error you should hit on a formula that will increase the number of revolutions that you generate on your shots.

Shoes

When it comes to purchasing your next pair of shoes, opt for quality, not price, when making your decision.

Footwork is important in bowling, and good footwear

aids footwork. The more games you bowl at one time, the more important it is to find a comfortable pair of shoes that will give you proper support.

Since the foot opposite your bowling arm slides while the other foot serves as an anchor, the bottoms of the two shoes differ. For a right-handed player, the right shoe is part leather, part rubber. The rubber bottom is ridged à la a basketball sneaker. It helps to grip the floor, which is especially welcome if you bowl in a center where the approaches tend to be slippery. The left shoe is all leather to help you slide.

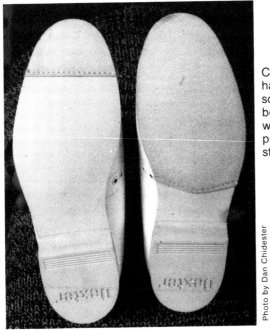

Custom-quality shoes have different bottoms so that one foot is better able to slide while the other provides added stability.

Photo by Dan Chidester

The better shoes have laces. The more eyelets, the greater the support.

There are cheaper shoes with the same slide sole on both feet. They can be used for either a righty or a lefty and, as such, are commonly purchased by bowling centers for rental to patrons.

You can buy a $30 pair and, if you're fortunate, get a

season or two out of them. My shoes have thousands of games in them and are still going strong. To save money tomorrow, spend some money today.

There is a wide variety of styles, including some that resemble sneakers. These are comfortable and look sharp but they tend not to have as much support. If you roll in events in which you bowl long blocks, you're better off purchasing a different type of shoe.

Contrary to popular misconception, the heel of the shoe (and not the sole) is what contributes more to a player either sliding or sticking. Nevertheless, by either roughing the sole or cleaning it you can affect how much you will slide. If your footwork is correct, the heel's effect will be the greater than that of the sole.

The better shoe lines feature a variety of heels. There are perforated soles which have a ribbed heel with holes. It decreases one's slide. That type of shoe is ideal for players like myself who prefer short slides. A lot of bowlers who are low to the ground on their release, like Marshall Holman, prefer long slides. If you are in that category, pick a smooth heel and a slide sole.

Personal preference rules here. You should know your game well enough to understand what will best suit your needs. For me, a slippery pair of shoes leaves me extremely unstable at the foul line. On the other hand, Marshall would probably be very unstable if he had to stop on a dime.

Most advanced players own both types. In fact, I, like many pros, carry three different pairs. More on that in a moment.

If you compete in different centers or at different times during the week at the same center, the condition of the approaches can vary. If the surfaces are very sticky, the smooth heel will counteract the approach. You'll find this to be a common problem on synthetic lane surfaces. That's because virtually all of today's shoes are designed for use on wood, not on plastic.

The opposite also holds: a slippery surface on which you might be more inclined to foul and/or injure yourself by falling can be rendered far less treacherous by using the perforated-style heel.

Like bowling balls, there are things that can be done to alter the characteristic of the shoe. If you use a piece of steel wool or a metal brush you can rough up the surface to decrease the amount that you will slide. I have seen a lot of players do this after stepping on something sticky, such as a puddle of water. In my opinion, that's probably the *worst* thing you can do. Instead, simply stand on the edge of the approach and rub your foot back and forth until your shoe feels comfortable.

If you step on something extremely sticky, such as a spot where a soft drink has been spilled, you may wish to use one of the aids sold in most pro shops. Rubbing some Teflon on the shoe also works. Take care not to get carried away, as excess Teflon could result in your sliding from the foul line to the parking lot!

A less-expensive trick is to rub cigarette ashes onto your shoe. Do NOT use powder. It tends to stick to the approach and becomes extremely dangerous to yourself and to your fellow bowlers. On top of that, it's also illegal.

Always test your sliding foot on the approach before making your next delivery. Sliding significantly more or less than you anticipate can result in an injury and/or a terrible shot.

The other danger is committing a needless foul. That could cost you a match. In the case of PBA star Mark Baker, sticking at the foul line deprived him of a strike and 20 pins on the score sheet during a 233–211 loss to Marshall Holman in the title game of the 1986 Firestone Tournament of Champions. One could make a case for that foul coming with a price tag to Mark of $22,000 and the winner's trophy of our sport's most prestigious title.

The lesson is that prior to bowling on a pair of lanes you should always inspect the foul line from gutter to gutter to discover if there are any problem areas that require attention. Remember to check your shoes prior to every shot.

As mentioned before, my equipment bag contains three

pairs of shoes. I have ones with real big rib heels that act almost like cleats. They have a black rubber bottom. That pair could probably stop a tractor trailer doing 55 miles per hour. I also have a regular perforated pair. Finally, I have nonperforated shoes which slide a lot.

Wrist Supports

Several support devices go on your bowling arm to secure your wrist into a specific position. Some of the newest ones are adjustable so that you can change the angle of your wrist.

Some varieties—like the Cobra and the Scorpion—are designed to increase the lift on your ball. Although it can be argued that they are producing a false roll, they do keep the wrist in a cupped position, which will greatly increase the number of revolutions on your ball. For individuals who have weaker wrists but still want to generate a big hook, this type of supporter comes in handy.

The Robbie and the Wrist Master are two products that maintain a straight wrist position. Because I have had past problems with wrist injuries, I wear one so as to avoid having my wrist support the entire weight of a 16-pound ball during portions of my delivery.

One common trait that all good wrist supports share is that they're easy to put on or remove quickly. PBA Hall of Famer Mike Durbin has used a cupped supporter for years for his strike shot. He removes it when shooting most types of spares that demand a straightened shot.

Wrist supports are usually of greatest help to many women and slighter-built men. Many smaller players use light balls because they think they're unable to handle something heavier. A good supporter allows you to increase the weight of your ball. Since doing so is a decided advantage (heavier balls deflect less when hitting the pocket), I'd recommend experimenting with these devices if you fall into this category.

Do not expect a wrist support to perform miracles. You won't gain any benefits if you bring your hand over the ball or throw a backup shot.

Rosin Bags

There are two basic types of rosin bags which are distinguishable by their color.

The yellow bag gets my vote. It dries your hand and fingers and isn't overly sticky. It leaves you with a good feel of the ball without being tacky. Some players will pat the yellow bag on top of the finger and/or thumb holes of their ball. Doing so should absorb any perspiration that is on the surface or is inside the holes.

The white powder bag is gummy. Use too much and you probably won't get out of the ball! Be careful when using it. Only pat it lightly with the tip of your fingers to get a better feel on the ball.

Remember that bowling regulations insist you wipe off all foreign substances from your ball, rosin included, prior to delivering your shot.

Towels

Every bowling bag should include a towel. I agree with Mike in highly recommending that you wipe off your ball before every shot, especially when rolling on oily or dirty lane surfaces. Failure to do so allows a buildup of foreign substances on your ball, which will decrease its gripping power. The result could be a lot of deflected shots which lessen carrying power.

In addition, towels come in handy to clean everything from dirt on the bottom of your shoes to sweat off of the top of your forehead (yes, even top-class pros get nervous on occasion!).

Tape

As you gain in ability, you must learn how to properly use tape. Every quality player I know employs it to full advantage. Using tape isn't just a good idea, it's a must for intermediate-level and advanced bowlers. I don't know of a single touring pro (either male or female) who doesn't use tape.

There is a common misconception among less-aware

After having stepped on any foreign substance, wipe off the bottom of your sliding foot's shoe with a towel.

Photo by Dan Chidester

players that your ball should always fit your hand as does your favorite pair of gloves. This fails to account for the fact that the diameters of your fingers and thumb are constantly changing. That ring that feels comfortable one day can seem tight or loose on other occasions.

On humid days, your hand swells. When it's cold, shrinkage occurs. As you bowl your thumb may swell or shrink. Slight changes in your body weight can also have a noticeable effect.

You cannot have a consistent and effective release unless you are able to grip the ball correctly. Your local pro should have drilled your thumb hole so it fits the *maximum* size of that digit.

When placed into the ball, your thumb should feel snug but not tight. I liken the grip of a ball to how one holds a parakeet. You want your grip to be tight enough that the bird won't fly away, yet sufficiently loose so as not to kill it.

The difference between a ball that feels just right and

one that causes you to squeeze just a little bit is minute, certainly not discernable to the naked eye. You have to learn how to recognize when your grip feels comfortable. The decision when to add or remove tape can be a major contributing factor toward your either winning or losing.

Some players prefer to place the tape so it rubs against the back of their thumb. To accomplish that, place the tape so it covers the six o'clock through nine o'clock positions for right-handed players and three through six o'clock spots for you southpaws.

My personal preference is to feel the tape against the inside of my thumb. That grip is gained by placing the tape between the noon and three o'clock spots. If you're left-handed, it's between nine o'clock and noon.

There are different types of tape on the market. I have a small hand which makes it harder for me to hold on to my ball. To give me the best grip possible I use tape underneath with a layer of Sure-Hook on top of it.

Sure-Hook is a product that is made of cork. The tape underneath is used for adjustment purposes. I can decrease the size of a thumb hole by adding a layer of tape under the Sure-Hook. The opposite is done by removing anywhere from one layer to all of the tape.

I would suggest not using a cork-type insert in the back of the hole, lest you rip the skin off that part of your thumb. It's not made to promote a clean release. I use it because I have very small hands so it helps me to better hold on to my ball.

Another option is to use a slick tape, such as the kind that electricians have, on the back part of the hole.

How you use tape is a matter of personal preference. I recommend experimentation during practice sessions. Through trial and error you will discover what feels most comfortable for your game.

Bowling Bags, Etc.

If you bring more than one ball to bowl, you should own a double bag. Since two balls plus your shoes and your other equipment will weigh around 35 pounds, I recommend getting a bag that features a shoulder strap. They're far easier to carry and are probably a bit more durable.

I suggest also owning an accessory bag for housing items such as your wrist supporters, tape, rosin bags, towel, and extra shoelaces.

If you bowl a lot of games, your hand and/or thumb becomes tender. Blisters and lost skin are common. That's also true when breaking in a new ball. Skin protector/Nu Skin is a must. These are alcohol-based liquids which, when combined with a patch or cotton, form a new layer of protection over the injured spot. They're quick-drying so they can be applied between frames.

Both cotton and patches are not without their shortcomings. The patch will grip your skin tightly. If it's applied near a joint it can pull and tear. While cotton has more "give," it is very difficult for the non-expert to apply. It has to be put on in an extremely thin layer.

To remove either, merely soak your hand in warm water or use nail polish remover.

Apparel

No longer does the bowling shirt resemble a potato sack with buttons. Today's bowling clothes are every bit as sharp as their counterparts for golf, tennis, or racquetball.

When selecting your bowling wardrobe, opt for function over fashion. Always wear a short-sleeved shirt that is sufficiently roomy so as not to restrict your armswing. Likewise, slacks should allow for a natural bend of the knee without offering any resistance.

Taking Care of Your Equipment

When you've invested a lot of hard-earned money to obtain the finest equipment available, make sure that you treat it properly. For example, do not leave your bowling ball(s) sitting in the trunk of your car in extreme weather. Hot days will soften their shells and turn that straight spare ball into a hooking monster. Cold weather will harden the shell and render that lovely strike ball into the straightest arrow this side of the Osmond family.

I've seen plastic balls that are left inside a car on a summer's day become considerably softer. Since the bowling center is heated at approximately 70 degrees the hardness of your ball's surface will actually change as you bowl. As that happens, the amount it will hook will also change. Bowling is tough enough without having to make frame-by-frame adjustments!

Take care of your bowling shoes the way you would your best pair of dress shoes. Likewise, treat your towel to an occasional washing and buy a new rosin bag before the old one is no longer useful.

7
MAKING THE MOST OF PRACTICE TIME

by Dave Ferraro

When it comes to practice habits, the typical bowler has a lot to learn from his counterparts in other sports. I can't imagine a serious golfer who doesn't spend time on the driving range or an intermediate-level tennis player who hasn't taken lessons.

Yet it's not uncommon for better-than-average bowlers to have horrible practice habits, if they practice at all. The majority of bowlers just bowl during league play. It wouldn't occur to them to practice or to take a lesson.

Those who do practice often just roll a few games and go home. Some don't even do that. They throw their strike ball and, if 10 pins don't go down, they hit the reset button instead of trying to convert the spare.

Maximizing your bowling potential requires precisely what getting the best out of your talents does in any other endeavor: hard work. Mike Aulby didn't win Bowler of the Year due to luck or being born with a gift. Only through hours and hours of practicing, doing the same things over and over again, was he able to develop his talents.

Too many players think they will be fine if they simply

buy a new ball and roll a few games per week. I assume that you are different.

For one thing, you have taken the time to read this book. That tells me that you are determined to improve. I hope what you have read so far has given you some insights. To put your increased knowledge to work, you will need to structure a practice session designed to remedy flaws in your game.

Before you arrive at the center, you should have some specific idea of what it is you want to accomplish. Perhaps you are having difficulty with cross-lane spares and you want to work on them, or your strike ball is hitting the pocket but not consistently carrying so you will attempt to improve your leverage at the foul line. Maybe your timing is giving you difficulty so you will be spending a session concentrating on coordinating your armswing with your footwork.

For *every* problem there is a solution. But *every* solution requires *purposeful* practice.

The key word is *purposeful*. I've heard it said that practice doesn't make perfect, practice makes *permanent*. That's 100 percent true. If you spend hours bowling with a serious flaw in your motion, that flaw will incorporate itself into your style.

Yes, there are several successful unorthodox players on today's PBA Tour. But the game's greatest stars, those who have enjoyed a number of outstanding years, are fundamentally sound. Good timing, a straight and unmuscled armswing, and a smooth delivery aren't prerequisites to becoming a good player but they sure do make it much easier.

Having said that, how do you go about structuring your practice session?

The first step I'd recommend is to take a few lessons from a highly respected local professional. Many PBA stars own or manage bowling centers and are available between tour seasons for instruction. There is a growing number of well-qualified house pros who can teach the game's finer points.

Having gotten yourself into the 150–190 average range, you obviously have a modicum of ability. Most players in the intermediate category have a big flaw (or two) that keeps them from reaching the next plateau. An instructor with a sharp eye can probably spot it and help you overcome it.

The First Step

Every practice session, just like when you're in a competitive setting, should start with a good warm-up. Gently stretch your legs, wrists, and bowling arm. Roll your first few shots at half speed.

Before working on the one area you wish to address, make sure you have thrown enough good shots to establish your personal rhythm. You cannot concentrate on improving one aspect of your delivery if everything else is out of whack. That's why you must engage in a good warm-up prior to getting down to serious business.

Concentration

Basically, there are two varieties of practice sessions. One option is to pick out a specific aspect of your game and work on improving it. I'll offer advice on that shortly.

The most common form is to simply bowl. Let's face it, ours is a sport in which repetition is key. Bowling does not demand the wide variety of athletic movements of basketball or soccer. To become good in our game requires acquiring muscle memory. By rolling hour after hour your body should become "locked into" your style. If that style is solid, you will noticeably improve.

There is one problem. Bowling for hours at a time gets boring. That's why you should limit the duration of any one session. When concentration lags you will get sloppy. At that point further play becomes counterproductive.

I'm always amazed that certain bowlers can work for long periods of time and maintain interest. The great Earl Anthony used to roll games for hours. When he felt too exhausted to continue, he would bowl another game and tell himself it was for a title. He was actually able to recreate the feeling of anxiety one feels when faced with a "must" strike situation in a significant match.

That Earl was able to do so speaks to his great mental strengths which were what separated him from mere mortals. I wish I could duplicate his ability to concentrate during practice sessions, but I can't.

Instead, my solution is to grab as good an opponent as I can find and compete with him. Even if the stakes are as low as a soft drink or a buck, the mere fact that I'm putting my skills to the test against someone else will fuel my competitive instincts.

I liken the difference between the two sessions to the way that many of my friends approach fitness. If they try jogging, after a few minutes they're aware of every little ache and pain. They run for a mile or two and quit.

But put the same person on a basketball court and he can play for hours at a time. That's because the ball and the opponent are like the proverbial carrot in front of the mule. Give me a person to compete against and I can concentrate far harder and longer than when practicing on my own.

As someone who bowls for his livelihood, I roll thousands of games a year. For a pro, practice usually represents little more than fine-tuning. We train to retain our muscle memory.

To you, the intermediate-level player, practice is different. There are surely aspects of your game that you must upgrade. Therefore, it's probably even more important to you than it is to a professional player that your session be well planned and executed.

The Purposeful Practice Session

The first step in designing a meaningful training scheme is to understand your own game. Just as a doctor can't write a prescription until he diagnoses the disease, you must identify an area of need before seeking the cure.

Once that's accomplished, concentrate exclusively on the one item you wish to upgrade. To successfully work on two things simultaneously is virtually impossible.

There are some exercises you can try that will prove helpful.

The dots game   The more serious you are about bowling, the greater the odds that you will find yourself competing in different centers with different oil patterns. There will be houses in which the shot with the highest percentage of carry and accuracy involves using an outside line and a fairly straight ball. Other centers are more rewarding to the big hook that is thrown from a deep inside line. Still others fall between the two extremes.

You will hit easy scoring conditions in which the player who strikes the most will win. You will also come across grind-'em-out places where the best spare shooter prevails.

There are two types of bowlers who have won tournaments on the PBA Tour. A "condition champion" is a guy who is a world-beater when he's playing on a surface that best suits his game. He might win this week and then not so much as cash in his next dozen events. Guys like this don't tend to last that long on the Tour.

Then there are "genuine" champions. These are the ones who are deadly on their favorite condition while no worse than very competitive under any other circumstance. I guarantee you that if the PBA holds next year's Firestone Tournament of Champions in the Sahara Desert, Mark Roth and Marshall Holman will still find a way to qualify for the top 24 match play. Their games are so fundamentally sound that they can post competitive scores on any oil pattern.

Bowling lore is filled with sad stories of "house champions" who are great at home but abysmal anywhere else. I know of one pro who has won eight regional tournaments, all rolled on house conditions. Under those circumstances, he can compete on even terms with the top bowlers in the world. However, when he tries the national PBA Tour he's as lost as a shark on sand. He's lucky if he can qualify for the main event out of the rabbit squad, much less earn any money.

To me, a player who has reached the intermediate level has shown that he or she is capable of becoming a good bowler. You ought to want to maximize your skills and then put them to the test in a competitive environment. If that's the case, you need to learn how to play a wide variety of strike shots.

The "dots game" is easily the best drill that I have come across toward helping you become a more versatile player. Of all the practice exercises my dad put me through during my developing years, none was as helpful.

As you know, there are seven dots across the approach (five boards apart). Each has a corresponding arrow out on the lane.

The objective of the dots game is to learn to strike using every conceivable angle. Start on the dot closest to the gutter on the side of your bowling hand. You must roll a set number of shots that hit the pocket.

Once that's accomplished, move to the next dot and repeat the procedure. As you go from your starting point of an outside line to the finishing point of a deep inside line, you will have to make adjustments in ball speed and hand position.

The outside line shot calls for greater speed and less hook. The deep inside position requires less speed coupled with more ball revolutions. Each time that you move five boards (one dot) to your left (to the right for a southpaw), your target should be altered in the same direction. Through experimentation you will discover how many boards yield the best results. An approximate ratio is one board on the lane for every two that you move with your feet.

Do not change bowling balls as you cross the lane. Yes, you could go to a softer-shell ball to help get the job done. By resisting that temptation you will force your body to learn to make adjustments. That will give you added options over the player who merely knows how to juggle equipment. For the serious bowler, more options equals more wins!

The dots game helps teach how to walk toward your target. If you are bellying your shot (letting it out several boards to the side of your bowling hand), walk in that direction. This will allow you to maintain a pendulum armswing that swings freely from your shoulder.

Do not become discouraged. The dots game is a very

The dots game is an excellent learning tool. Notice how Dave must vary his target to compensate for changing his position at the foul line.

difficult exercise. Even after years of practice, many pros still have trouble with certain types of shots. However, the top bowlers are smart enough to realize that by becoming no less than competent on their least-favorite shot they will stand a far better chance at reaching their goals.

Even if I can't beat an Amleto Monacelli or a Mark Baker very often when conditions favor the power player, I can at least do well enough to finish in the top 24. I know that I can go to town when a straighter shot is in vogue.

Having said that, there is a big difference between becoming versatile and trying to be something that you're not. A lot of bowlers have gotten in trouble when they've attempted to stray beyond their natural games.

Don Genalo is a case in point. Using a very direct line to the pocket coupled with marvelous accuracy, from 1983 through 1986 he finished among the top 20 money winners each year. During that time Don earned just under $300,000. In 1987 he noticed that the crankers were dominating.

Don decided to change his game to get more power. In doing so he lost the qualities that had made him successful. That year he earned only $28,970. When he went back to his natural style in 1988 he reestablished himself as one of the top performers on the Tour.

Doubling the dots challenge   As you become more proficient at playing various lines, challenge yourself. Raise the number of pocket hits that must be achieved before you can move to the next dot. Or move only after a specific amount of strikes. For an added test, move only after a set number of *consecutive* pocket hits or strikes.

Another option is to play the equivalent of basketball's around-the-world. Change positions by one dot after each frame. When you roll high scores under that stipulation you have truly become a versatile player. You are now prepared to compete on any lane condition that can be thrown at you.

A few words of advice   The name of the game toward improvement is *trial and error*. Practice is the time to learn how to change hand positions, alter ball speed, cover difficult spares, and juggle equipment. When you're bowling in league play or in a tournament there is little room for experimentation.

Don't take false pride in your practice scores. There are countless "training session terrors" who are always telling their teammates how they rolled a 650 series the other afternoon. Big deal. What I want to know is how you will perform under pressure when it counts.

Nice scores are nice achievements. But they don't count for a thing unless you leave that practice session a better bowler than when you walked into that center a few hours before.

Spare Shooting

As I noted in our segment on shooting spares and splits, there are no hard and fast rules as to where you must stand or aim. However, keep in mind that *all* of the game's premiere spare shooters aim cross-lane at corner pins, roll their ball hard and straight on all attempts not involving double wood, and concentrate on every shot (no matter how simple it may appear). Remember, too, that all your motions should be directed at your target and your armswing should be straight.

If you know the proprietor, he may allow you to shadow bowl (roll shots without pins). Even with a full deck, you can still aim for a specific pin.

A good way to get your money's worth from a practice session while improving your accuracy is to shoot the same spare on several consecutive shots. An alternative is to do that with the first ball of every frame and then roll your strike shot on the second delivery.

Force yourself to stick with it. Learn to master your "worst" spare. Let's say the 10 pin is your usual downfall. Challenge yourself. Bowl until you have covered five in a row. That's not as hard as it sounds.

The biggest problem is often a lack of confidence. Once you discover that you *can* make that spare, you *will* start to make it far more often. There is no easier time to learn how to convert it than in practice when the peer pressure to perform isn't present.

Despite that, all of us love the feeling of seeing ten pins flying into the pits. There's no better moment in bowling than when you get that *X*.

It's tempting to only roll strike shots. I must admit that's exactly what I did in my younger days. I'd roll my first ball. If I didn't strike I would hit the reset button. Since I've begun to work on my spare shooting in practice I have improved markedly on that very important aspect of my game. I can honestly say that I never could have won three titles in 1988 just on the strength of the number of strikes I threw.

Use the "Wrong" Equipment to Get the Right Results

With today's wide variety of superb bowling balls, it's very tempting to let the equipment do the work for you. If you want to roll a powerful hook ball it's easier to buy an ultra-soft-shell urethane ball than it is to perfect your hand release. There's just one problem: sooner or later you'll hit a condition that even the best equipment can't overcome. At that point the player with the superior release will prevail.

One of the best ways to improve any aspect of your release is to use the exact opposite equipment that you would select in a match. Want to learn how to roll the ball straighter? Then pick a ball that hooks a lot. If you can learn to roll that soft-surface ball more directly, think how straight your shots will travel when you go to a hard shell.

Do you want to increase your ball's revolutions and hitting power? Try a hard-shell ball that is very difficult to hook (an old rubber ball works great). That will force you to roll the ball slowly and hit on your release.

Before ending the session, go back to the ball you will use in that situation during competition. It's important that you get accustomed to its feel since no two balls can be drilled exactly alike. You will be amazed at the difference you will find from the start of the session.

Ball Speed

Once a player gets that great feeling of being "locked in," it's a challenge to keep it. At that point, repetition is all that matters. The good amateur can probably roll up to a half dozen shots the same way. A top pro can do it for several games.

One of the key factors is the ability to maintain nearly the same ball speed. When Bob Benoit won $100,100 for rolling a televised perfect game in the title match of the 1988 Quaker State Open, he did it with remarkably consistent trajectory. The differential between Bob's fastest and slowest shots that game was an amazing 0.13 of a second (2.56 to 2.69). His last 10 strikes were within 0.07 of a second of each other!

That level of control is extraordinary. The results of being able to maintain the same ball speed speak for themselves. No matter how you slice it, one can't improve on perfection.

The chances are that maintaining the same speed is the result of a smooth delivery and ideal timing. A good way to test yourself is to have a friend time you with a stopwatch. To translate your speed from time (the measure of how long it takes for your ball to go from the foul line to the headpin) to miles per hour, use the chart in Chapter 2.

Practice rolling strike shots at different speeds. The trick is to be able to roll a powerful and accurate ball at both a slow (15 miles per hour) and a high (20 miles per hour) speed.

Lofting   Learning to loft your shots out *onto* the lane rather than dropping the ball *into* the lane is a prerequisite of throwing an effective strike ball. Except for Larry Laub, I can't name a single bowler who fashioned a successful career by laying the ball short.

You should be able to lift your shot toward your target. Do not roll it on the foul line or heave it upward. In time, you must learn how to get your shot at least a couple of feet out onto the lane.

To work on your lofting technique, place a towel one foot or two past the line.

Photo by Dan Chidester

An effective practice tool is to place a towel just past the foul line. Have it extend six inches to a foot onto the lane. As you feel more comfortable lofting your shots you can place the towel further out onto the lane. Two feet is a pretty good distance for most players.

Release your shot so the ball hits beyond the towel. Chances are that you will kill two birds with one stone since the towel will force you to produce a good follow-through.

It is permissible to loft shots farther. Mark Roth and Brian Voss can comfortably get their balls to land at the dots on the lane when conditions call for such a shot. The key is that they do that naturally and *never* get distance as a result of hitting the ball on the upswing.

Make sure that the ball leaves your hand when both are moving parallel to the lane.

Go to a House That's Not Your Home

I strongly recommend that once you have honed your basic game you practice at several different centers. Each house has slightly different characteristics. Learning to conquer a variety of bowling establishments can't help but increase your versatility.

Even if all of the centers in your area have the same oil pattern, the lanes could have different characteristics. My family owns two bowling centers: Mid City Lanes (in Kingston, New York) and Southern Dutchess Bowl (Beacon, New York). Although they are oiled the same, my shot reacts very differently. Mid City's lanes don't hook back nearly as much as at Southern Dutchess.

The reason is that there are other ways that lanes can vary besides the oil pattern. The wood can be a bit harder or older. One place might be cooler or warmer than where you are accustomed to bowling. Whatever the reason, practicing at different centers will help you learn bowling's little tricks.

For example, the strike ball that works at Place A may leave a weak 10 pin at Place B. So you move a half board to the right. The strike at A could be a solid 10 pin at B. So you move forward or backward a few inches at the start of your approach.

Very often it's those little things that can make a big difference in a big match, which is why good practice habits will give you an invaluable competitive edge.

Coaching

Tom Watson doesn't make a shot without his caddy. If Michael Jordan gets in a scoring slump he can spend hours with his coach studying his jump shot in slow motion on videotape. Darryl Strawberry enjoys unlimited time in the batting cage under the watchful eye of his team's hitting instructor.

Many pros are available to give lessons. You can call the PBA, LPBT, or ABC for the names of the top teachers in your area.

Photo by Dan Chidester

For some reason, bowlers are different. Except for pros and the rare amateur player, very few have personal coaches. Yet a coach is a great asset. He can spot mistakes that would otherwise go undetected and become a part of your delivery.

A VCR is also a great asset. There is no substitute for watching yourself in action.

Not surprisingly, many of the best teaching pros combine instruction with videotape. The combination of coaching and taping helped me to escape one of my worst slumps. Somehow, my backswing had gotten well out of alignment. It kept deteriorating until it reached a point where it was virtually nonexistent. Not only was it too short, it wrapped behind my back. My unrestricted pendulum armswing had given way to a muscled delivery.

When I came home from the Tour, my brother, Steve, and my dad, Jack, needed all of about three shots to analyze my problem. "I can't believe it," Steve said in a voice that sounded shocked. "You've got no backswing!" By looking at the VCR I discovered exactly what he meant. A few *purposeful* practice sessions later, a correction was in place and my slump had ended.

Feel free to fully exploit modern technology to upgrade your skills.

8
COMPETITION
PREPARATION
by Mike Aulby

As does any other athlete, the good bowler prepares in advance to compete. This is one of the many "little things" you should do. It's important just like having a good pre-shot routine and being in shape are significant. When you acquire all of the small good habits of the serious player, you will gain a considerable advantage over many opponents.

Before I roll my first warm-up shot there are a number of things I do to give myself the best chance I can of being successful.

First, I do some scouting. By watching the previous squad bowling I can get some idea of how the lanes should be played. I look for a bowler whose game is similar to mine to see what he is doing. That may offer an important clue. If he's found something that works, I might try the same thing with my first practice shots. That gives me a good starting point during warm-ups when all 10 practice shots are a valuable commodity.

Before stepping onto the lane, I make sure that every ball in my bag fits my hand. That involves a lot of inserting or removing of tape. I want to make certain that I can make an

Your chances of producing a solid performance are increased by purposeful preparation.

Photo by Frank Valeri

immediate equipment change to any ball I might wish by having everything prepared in advance.

The next step is to stretch. For some reason, the over-whelming majority of league players neglect this aspect of warming up. I can't imagine a participant in any other sport not engaging in a loosening-up routine.

The legs should be stretched as should your neck, back, shoulders, and the wrist of the bowling hand. The latter is very important to prevent injury. Far too many players experience wrist problems because they fling their initial warm-up shots without having done any stretching.

I bend my wrist backward, holding it in an extended position for five to ten seconds. I then bend it forward for the same period of time. I also do some upper body twists to help loosen and relax my muscles.

Along with the physical advantage of having my body ready to perform, I also feel more mentally alert for having engaged in moderate exercise before bowling.

Stretch a variety of muscles prior to rolling that first warm-up shot.

Photo by Dan Chidester

Prior to my initial shot, I slide my foot from gutter to gutter in front of the foul line on both lanes. I make certain that my shoes and the approaches are clear of any sticky and/or slippery substances.

When it comes time to roll practice balls, your body should be ready to perform. Nevertheless, it's a good idea to take it easy on your first shot. This, too, could help prevent a possible injury. The more of a power player you are, the more important it is that you exercise caution on your first shot or two.

For me, my body is so attuned to constant bowling that I am able to produce 100 percent effort on my first ball. In that regard, I'm luckier than a lot of pros who need a couple of rolls before they're ready to go to work.

Having analyzed what I learned about the lane conditions by witnessing the previous squad, I have a pretty fair idea about what ball and line will work best. I try that combination first.

Although my pinfall doesn't count, I view this shot as every bit as important as if a game were riding in the balance. That's because I need to execute a good delivery and hit my

Notice Dave's level of concentration after he's released his shot as he warms up before the championship round of a PBA tournament.

Photo courtesy of the PBA

target if I am to glean any useful information about the lane and how to best play it.

If I find something that's working, I will roll a few shots using that line. I may also experiment with another ball and/or angle to give me an alternative backup strategy in case what is working now breaks down later as the lanes change.

I always include two cross-lane corner pin shots during my warm-up period. That means shooting both the 7 and the 10 pins. That is important for two reasons.

First, since converting spares is a vital aspect of winning, they shouldn't be neglected. Many a match has been lost by a player blowing a corner pin leave because the lane hooked either a lot more or a lot less than anticipated. Any surprises the house has in store for you should be uncovered when a miss doesn't spell disaster.

Second, you can find out a lot about the lane condition this way. It's important that I know whether the lanes are evenly oiled from gutter to gutter. I closely monitor how my ball reacts to determine if the middle of the lane is wet, dry, or somewhere between the two extremes.

Do not save these two conversions for the very end of practice. I suggest making sure that you have a few warm-up balls remaining. Should you miss, you will then have another attempt at them in practice. That's important for both finding the groove and gaining needed confidence.

I'm not a big advocate of watching other players during my warm-up period. Perhaps I might learn something from observation but I'm more concerned with concentrating on my own game. Only if you are totally lost would I suggest looking around to see what others are doing.

While bowling represents my livelihood and the warm-up period is very important, I still look at it as an enjoyable experience. Whether a person is a PBA pro or a once-a-week recreation player, bowling is still a game and should be fun.

I've heard many of my peers say they'll quit the game when it stops becoming fun and starts becoming work. That may sound like an odd perspective for a professional player, but it shows that to be successful in any endeavor it certainly helps to enjoy what you are doing.

The smile or good-natured kidding you engage in before a match can help put you at ease. That's especially true if you are prone to becoming nervous in what you perceive to be an important match. Just don't get so carried away with levity that you lose concentration on the task at hand.

Confidence Is Key

One of two things can happen during your warm-up. Either you will do very well or you'll bomb out. Treat both circumstances as having little effect on what's to come.

Poor shooting in practice isn't recommended but it isn't fatal, either. Many a time I stunk in warm-up only to perform up to my potential once the action began for real. Rather than becoming discouraged, I concentrate even harder to uncover both my problem and the appropriate solution.

There is *always* an answer to your problem, whether it's a lack of concentration, a physical mistake, the wrong equipment, or playing the wrong line (or any combination of these). It's up to you to determine that answer as quickly as possible.

It's equally important not to start foaming at the mouth after booming some strikes in practice. Not only could the added adrenaline give you fast feet and sweaty palms, you can become mentally unglued.

I never tell myself something like "I'm going to average 240 today." I've found that when I think too far ahead like that I get into trouble. No matter how "hot" you think you are, you can only roll one strike at a time. Take every shot as it comes, concentrating fully on just the upcoming delivery.

A Little Common Sense Never Hurts, Either

Being mentally and physically prepared to the best of your ability from the first shot through the last is vital. I'm shocked how many league bowlers either neglect their warm-up altogether or are very slipshod in their approach.

A significant percentage of intermediate-level bowlers often show up at the lanes either late or just as practice begins. They rush to get on their shoes and hurriedly toss a shot or two. When competition starts, they haven't a clue about what the lanes are doing. Moreover, they aren't physically ready to perform.

Between PBA seasons I bowl as a substitute in some Indianapolis-area leagues. I always arrive at the center well before the starting time. So should you.

Once there, check your equipment, observe the previous league's bowlers, stretch your body, and be ready to go when the gun sounds. It's always far better to arrive 15 minutes early than 15 seconds late.

You can keep track of how effectively you have been warming up by keeping tabs on how your seasonal average for your first game contrasts with games two and three. Also note how many spares and strikes you get in the first three frames as compared to all others.

Although it may not seem that way, pinfall counts just as

much in the first frame as it does in the tenth. You will feel more confident if you are fully prepared to compete every time a match begins. That, in turn, will also help you perform better.

Injury Prevention

There is a final but very important bonus to adequate preparation: injury prevention.

Dave has told me that during his early years he didn't bother to stretch before bowling. He paid a big price for that transgression, having suffered tendonitis in his right (bowling) wrist. It became so bad that it sidelined him from several tournaments during his best year (1988). That might have cost him being named Bowler of the Year. More importantly, the injury threatened to end his career.

Photo by Dan Chidester

Taping the wrist has helped Dave overcome tendonitis.

Fortunately, proper diagnosis and rehabilitation allowed him to recover. He now engages in a precompetition routine that begins with a thorough stretching regimen that includes various wrist exercises. Dave then tapes his wrists and lower arm to provide extra support.

As he begins his warm-up shots, he's careful to roll the first few shots gently onto the lane. It's not until he is loose that he powers through his release and lofts his shots. These precautions have helped to keep him healthy.

It all boils down to your self-image. If you think of bowling as a sport and yourself as an athlete, you will prepare to compete in a serious and intelligent manner. Consider those 15 minutes prior to the start of play as a great opportunity to gain an edge on those of your fellow bowlers who neglect this aspect of the game.

As in any endeavor, the better prepared you are for the upcoming task, the more likely you are to perform to the best of your ability.

9
THE MENTAL GAME
by Dave Ferraro

The more advanced level of competitive bowling you reach, the greater will become the importance of your mental game. In the professional circuit the ability to concentrate is even more of a factor in winning or losing as the physical game.

Put 160 pros on a soft condition and they'll all strike virtually at will. Place those same players on a more challenging pair of lanes with a lot at stake and it won't take long to separate the contenders from the pretenders.

I've heard veteran NFL placekicking star Matt Bahr claim that there must be hundreds of athletes who can boot footballs as well as he can when in an empty stadium. But put a game on the line with seventy thousand roaring fans and Matt is the calmest man in the stadium. The ability to think analytically when under duress and to overcome the pres-. sure is what makes Matt Bahr so special.

It's the same on the PBA and LPBT Tours. In my opinion, the mental game is probably the number one criterion for winning when your average is at or above 200. For the 175-average player it's probably 50 percent concentration and 50 percent physical. The lower the average you have, the

Photo by Frank Valeri

The mental game helps separate champions, like Mike Aulby and Steve Cook, from also-rans.

greater the importance of physical execution.

Despite that, the majority of players at all plateaus fail to reach their potential because their mental game is deficient. If you don't recognize and learn from your mistakes you will never get beyond a certain level. On the other hand, the player who thinks his way through all situations will gain 10–20 pins per game.

I trace most of my improvement to gaining confidence and a different perspective. In the early years of my pro career I would come off a bad block thinking I had bowled poorly. When I fail to score now I always think, "it's not me." That doesn't mean that I played the lanes correctly or selected the right equipment. It does mean that I feel I didn't roll the ball badly.

Why is that important? In the "old days" when my scores were subpar I wouldn't be thinking about possible adjustments. Instead, I'd be questioning aspects of my delivery. Before long, the physical "corrections" made things go from bad to worse.

Although there are days when I bowl better than on other occasions, I never come off of the lanes thinking "I didn't throw the ball well today."

The reality of the PBA Tour is that being properly lined up with the optimum piece of equipment for that condition yields more area with which to work on your strike ball. While the pro may not knock 'em dead on an off day, he will remain competitive.

One of the keys to success on the PBA Tour is to stay in the hunt during the days and weeks when you aren't razor sharp. That's why the genuine stars spend little time questioning their own games and a lot of time trying to figure out equipment and strike line solutions.

Hold That Temper

The number one item in the easier-said-than-done category involves maintaining your composure. In my younger days I allowed myself to become upset when I got bad breaks and/ or my opponent received good luck. With a bit of maturity came the realization that misplaced anger is counterproductive. You can't think clearly when you're mad. And not thinking clearly for even a frame or two can be very costly.

If you bowl you *will* leave ringing 10 pins. There *will* be games in which you toss a seemingly perfect shot only to have the 8 pin stand up and laugh in your face. There *will* also be occasions when you hit the pocket five times in a row with nothing to show for it and your rival gets a triple as his middle strike cuts through the nose or goes Brooklyn.

It all comes with the territory, and it all evens out in the long run if you don't let it destroy you first. While there isn't a pro bowler who doesn't understand that, you'd be amazed how many times we still blow our cool when competing in a tournament. In fact, there are legitimate PBA stars who I can virtually guarantee will fall apart in a game when Lady Luck doesn't go their way. They will allow one unlucky hit to affect their concentration which, in turn, causes several more bad shots.

The worst case I saw occurred in the second frame of a tournament. One of the Tour's better-known power players left back-to-back taps. He got disgusted and, for all intents and purposes, quit. He became so unnerved that he didn't hit the pocket for several frames, nor did he even seem to care.

It's hard to imagine someone treating his livelihood in such an immature fashion. That's why I don't think the player in question will ever amount to much on the Tour unless he grows up—which is a shame because he's blessed with a lot of talent. However, physical talent without a similar level of mental ability doesn't get one very far.

If you can control your temper as much as possible, you will suffer far fewer bad shots due to being upset. From a personal perspective, I bowl a lot better when I'm able to remain low-key. It's the same with Mike. We try to approach tournaments on a frame-by-frame basis, regardless of the results of our preceding frame(s) or game(s).

Even though we both run out the occasional important shot, by the time we sit down we have also cooled down. When we are able to remain on an even keel we usually do our best.

However, not everyone is like us. There are players who are at their best when they're emotionally hyped up. Among those who quickly come to mind are Marshall Holman, Ernie Schlegel, and Pete Weber. If they had to bowl low-key they would probably struggle. You must be true to your personality although you can't ever totally lose your composure even if you are the fired-up type.

Confidence Is Critical

Like the little train that could, believing you are capable of performing under pressure is at least half the battle. Prior to capturing my first PBA title in 1986 I always *thought* I was probably capable of winning a national event. After I beat John Gant in the championship match, 254–221, to win the Budweiser Classic in Columbus, I *knew* I could do it again.

Before that game I had made a few televised finals

without any success. Until I got over that hump I couldn't become the player that I am today.

Knowing you can win is a lot bigger boost than merely thinking you can win. Before my first title I felt a little bit inferior to the top pros. After that I cashed the following week during the final Tour stop of 1986. I began the 1987 Winter Tour by making the top 24 match play finals in six of the year's first seven tournaments.

I never made three in a row before in my previous four full years on the Tour. The difference wasn't a physical improvement. It was all a matter of confidence.

The pendulum swings both ways. I've seen some of the game's finest talents go into miserable slumps. What often happens is they have a bad week or two and overreact.

After failing to cash on conditions not conducive to their style, they make major changes when all that's needed is some fine-tuning. When they finally get on their condition— the one on which they would normally dominate—they are so out of whack that they aren't even competitive.

Keeping a positive attitude and not panicking when things don't go your way is even tougher for left-handed players. There are events on the Tour when a southpaw is at a great disadvantage due to the lane condition.

They don't get a shot every week. The better ones cash most of the time under adverse circumstances. But there are oil patterns on which a lefty simply can't win. Take, for example, the 1987 U.S. Open when every penny of the $500,000 prize fund went to the righties. The following year's tourney saw the top lefty, Johnny Petraglia, finish 60th. Out of one million bucks in two years the lefties collected $1,500. Something like that can be extremely discouraging.

Right-handed players are in such a majority that there will always be a good number of us making the show and the top 24, regardless of the condition.

That's why a lefty can get a false read on the source of his difficulties. It's hard for them to determine if they are at fault or if it's simply a case of the lanes not being playable from their side.

To a lesser extent, the same can be said for specific styles of players. There are conditions that favor crankers and others that are more advantageous to strokers. The key, for pros and serious amateurs, is to be no less than competitive on your least favorite condition and to go to town when the lanes are to your liking.

Of one thing you can be sure: sooner or later you will hit a slump. Aside from not panicking, you also must avoid the temptation to blame everyone else for your difficulties.

There are a couple of very good strokers on the PBA circuit who have fallen on hard times of late. I have literally heard them bellyaching after the initial six-game block of a tournament. In terms a bit stronger than those in a family-oriented instructional book, someone will say, "Son of a gun, the crankers have it all this week."

They'd be far better advised to spend half as much energy finding a solution as they spend looking for a scapegoat. The name of the game in bowling is to solve the

Photo courtesy of the PBA

Bowling superstar Marshall Holman can and has won from a variety of angles.

condition. That's what makes it such a challenging game and so rewarding to those who conquer adversity.

The player who can play only the tenth board is pretty limited. It's people like Pete Weber, Brian Voss, Dave Husted, Marshall Holman, and Mark Roth who can win playing anywhere from the 5, 15, and 20 boards who are the genuine stars. They're tough to beat even when they're not on their winning condition.

There isn't as much as you might imagine that separates a good many "condition champions" from the genuine stars. A significant amount of the difference is mental. Only a small fraction of it usually relates to a disparity in physical ability.

The guy who wins from 5, 15, and 20 boards believes he can do it. The top players expect to do well each and every time out. That's one of the main reasons they do succeed. When Marshall Holman loses he gets mad. He doesn't feel content just to have cashed in the middle of the pack because the condition wasn't to his liking.

I try to take the attitude that, while I might not be able to win on all conditions, I should be able to make money on anything the PBA lane maintenance crew can dish up. Yes, there will be weeks when I will be shut out. Hopefully, on those occasions I can continue to work hard so that I can learn from my mistakes.

There are tournaments in which every pro finds himself entering the last block of qualifying knowing he doesn't have a chance of cashing. Some withdraw from the event. Others go through the motions on the lanes. The real competitors continue to give 100 percent effort.

Even if there is no hope of a financial reward for doing well, good players know that a good block could boost their confidence heading into next week's tournament. Maybe they will learn something about that condition that will give them an edge the next time they find themselves bowling on a similar oil pattern.

Moreover, there is a certain feeling of satisfaction one can derive from knowing you gave it your best shot from the first ball through the last while others were packing it in. As of this writing, I have withdrawn from only one tournament in my entire career, and that was due to an injury. ·

Every time you step onto a lane you should learn something. You can't always control whether you will score well or not, but you *can* control your attitude. No loss is a defeat unless you failed to learn something that will help you in the future.

Never let one game ruin your night or your tournament. It's quite common for Tour newcomers to shoot a few big games followed by a 150. At the first sign of trouble they fall apart. One poor score leads to several more terrible games.

Out of a 42-game tournament, even the most successful of the stars knows he won't produce 42 scores with which he's satisfied. The trick is to grind out the best of the bad situations so you don't beat yourself. Once you've thrown the last shot of a bad game you must consider it ancient history. Forget about it and concentrate on what you must do to make your next shot a good one.

When you are in a tournament whose format calls for you to change pairs after each game you will hit some on which scoring will be low. If you get 170 while the other guy shoots 150 you are up the same amount as when you triple in the tenth to roll 210 to his 190. Don't just bear down in the final frames of good games. The pins you pick up in the tenth frame of a grindout game count just as much as the ones at the end of a big score.

Few people like bowling on lanes 1 and 2 or the highest-numbered pair in a house with that intimidating wall right on your shoulder. It isn't as much fun to roll on lanes whose oil patterns run contrary to your game. Nevertheless, the real competitor relishes such situations as a challenge. He knows that there is special satisfaction to be won if he can overcome those handicaps.

I've said it before and I'll say it a million times again: bowling is all about solving the condition. It's about what you have to do to get the most pins, even if that means throwing a straight ball à la Amleto Monacelli at the 1988 Showboat Invitational. Do whatever it takes to succeed.

The Greater the Pressure, the More You Must Think Positively

It's the last frame of a close game and your opponent is on the approach first. Which of the following are you thinking?

A. I hope he opens so we win.

B. I hope he doesn't double so I only need a mark to win.

C. I hope he strikes out so I can strike out to beat him.

Give me the option and I'll pick C every time. So should you.

If you have that attitude, you stand a far greater chance of performing well in pressure situations. The guy who selects A is in big trouble when his opponent doesn't self-destruct. The only reason he hopes his rival won't do well is because he doesn't think he can come through with the key shot.

The reason you are competing is you relish the challenge of putting yourself to the test. The supreme test of a bowler at any level is having to produce in the clutch. That's where the fun of the game lies. If you don't want to put yourself to the test you should limit your bowling to a so-cially-oriented mixed league.

No, you won't come through in the clutch every time. You may not even succeed the majority of the time. Nevertheless, you should still want to be placed in those situations. It's very important to have a positive approach.

I want to be placed in that situation where I need a strike, or a few strikes to win. Sometimes I mess up. At least I had the fun of trying.

It sure is satisfying when you do come through (and what a confidence booster it can be!). When I bowled in the championship round of the 1987 Miller Lite Open I struck out to win the first two games. I breezed through the semifinal match to earn the right to meet top-seeded Brian Voss for the title.

Brian struck out in the tenth for a 204 game. I needed a

double to win. Having won but one title up to that point, I had never been in that situation before. I stuffed both shots because I thought I could and I wanted to be placed in that situation. After it was all over it sure felt extra good, a lot better than if I'd won because Brian had opened.

Bowling's all-time greats relish the spotlight. Dick Weber says he's a ham, so he loves needing to produce to win. That's precisely why he's the only man in the sport's history to have won a PBA title in four different decades. Mark Roth exudes an air of unbridled confidence that he will come through. His attitude can unnerve less confident opponents.

The only man to capture at least one PBA title in four different decades, Hall of Famer Dick Weber thrives on performing while under pressure.

Photo courtesy of the PBA

One way of thinking positively is to remind yourself how many times you've done what is required in that situation. Let's say you need a strike for the win. Perhaps you've never rolled a pressure-packed strike before. But you certainly have gotten more strikes in your life than you can count. Tell yourself, "If I could do it then, I can do it now." Close your eyes for a second and picture yourself rolling that perfect shot.

One reason that Mark Roth is one of only two men to win over 30 national PBA titles is his unbridled confidence.

Photo courtesy of the PBA

Block out all distractions. Hell, you know you can do it! You've already won half the battle because you are thinking in the most productive manner.

Another positive approach is to concentrate on executing something that's under your control. In bowling, you can roll a good shot and not be rewarded with a strike. Perhaps you have a history of "choking."

If that's the case, don't get up for that critical shot thinking, "Oh Lord, I need a strike!" Instead, tell yourself that your objective is simply to make a good shot. Just think about what you must do to execute properly. If you then leave a ringing 10 pin you can take satisfaction in knowing that you didn't succumb to the pressure. By doing that, you will see that you've made some improvement. In turn, that will build confidence. In time you will start getting those big strikes.

Don't expect overnight miracles. It took me years to get to the point where I'm able to think on the right track when under pressure. I know there is no guarantee that I'll be able to maintain that outlook should I hit a prolonged dry spell.

Don't think for a minute that I haven't squandered my share of pressure-filled matches. I'd be lying if I pretended otherwise. It even occurred during 1988, my best year on tour. Entering the position round game of match play, all I needed to qualify for the next day's televised finals was to lose by less than 20 pins to Brian Voss.

Early in the game I missed a 4 pin to the left when I bounced my ball during my release. Worried about making the same mistake when faced with another 4 pin toward the end of the match, I missed it to the right. That's because my mind was playing tricks on me due to the previous mistake in that situation.

In the preceding 41 games I converted every 4 pin situation. Now, with a shot at the big money on the line, I was blowing successive attempts. My mind caused my body to make a physical mistake.

If a pro's confidence is subject to being shaken, don't expect that you won't have to fight periods when you are doubting yourself. Just remind yourself at those times that the best way to make a good shot is to think you will do so.

Pressure affects us all. Don't be kidded into thinking pros don't perceive the same fears you do. Come to a triple-crown event and then attend a run-of-the-mill tournament. You will notice a big difference in our attitudes. You can bet your paycheck that we are all a lot more uptight when the prestige and prize money increase.

The key isn't to pretend pressure doesn't exist. The key is to know it's there and relish it as an added challenge to be overcome.

There's no defense in bowling so why watch your opponent?!   With the exception of golf and some sports in which judges determine the outcome (i.e., gymnastics, diving, and figure skating), in all other sports you can mount a defense to counter your opponent's offense.

The only "defense" in bowling is to strike so often that the less-confident opponent chokes. Short of that, there isn't a thing you can do to minimize his score other than resorting to bad sportsmanship. As such, there really is no reason to watch him bowl.

Just worry about your game. That was an important factor when I won my first title.

Just before the last 8-game block of match play on Friday night, my dad suggested that I not even look at my opponent or the scoreboard. He told me to keep my mind focused on what I had to do on my upcoming delivery to produce the best shot I could.

Dad's advice worked. I won my first seven matches that night and breezed to a 200+ gap over my nearest rival. I entered the title round as the top seed.

Who Sneezed?

Leave rabbit ears to rabbits (the furry variety, not the guys who have to qualify on Mondays for PBA events). It's easy to hear every pin that drops. I'm at my best when I'm totally attuned to my game. Athletes in all sports refer to that phenomenon as being in "the zone." You are so focused on the task at hand that you wouldn't notice if Madonna and Sean Penn were fighting on the next lane.

When I'm bowling my best I have tunnel vision. I don't see a distraction no matter what it is. I don't think about where I'm going for lunch after I bowl or what the standings might be. I am not the least bit concerned about the crowd's reaction or that some phone's ring is barely audible.

On the other hand, when I'm bowling badly I see and hear every little thing. I notice that this guy has tossed down his towel in disgust and that guy is cursing under his breath.

Getting into a state of mind of deep concentration is invaluable in every walk of life. That holds just as true for a lawyer writing a brief as it does for Michael Jordan when he's on the foul line. If I could stay in that zone all of the time I would never lose another tournament. The same can be said for virtually any of the top 50 PBA pros.

Unfortunately, when you're bowling for long periods of

time it's not humanly possible to achieve that state. That doesn't mean we can't strive to do that. Just think of the progress you would make if you could merely double the number of games during which you are fully concentrating.

If you want a role model, pick my coauthor   There are many pros who possess great mental games. Few, if any, are better than Mike Aulby.

I have never seen him kick a ball return, curse, or even break a pencil. I have never heard him complain about the lane condition. That's absolutely amazing given that there were many occasions when he and his fellow lefties had a legitimate grievance.

He doesn't get distracted by fans or fellow bowlers.

Maintaining your composure, even when big money and prestige are on the line, is a must.

Your teammates always need you to contribute When you are bowling in a league, you are part of a team. If you kick the rack after missing you won't do much to help your teammates' concentration or confidence.

Encourage each other at all times and never give up. Don't ever give the opposing team the satisfaction of seeing you get down, even if you can't seem to hit the ocean.

Think of your attitude as contagious. If you redouble your determination to be positive and to vocally support your teammates even when you are struggling, you can make a valuable contribution. Besides, the mark a guy gets in the tenth frame of a 140 game counts just as much as the spare his teammate rolls for a 190.

At the end of the year, it isn't Joe Smith who won the league; it's his team that won. In league play, bowling is a team game, and your mental approach should treat it that way.

APPENDIX A

GLOSSARY

Arrows: Series of seven triangular designs $14\frac{1}{2}$–$15\frac{1}{2}$ feet past the foul line which are placed every fifth board across the lane to serve as aiming points for shots.

Axis weight: Method of ball drilling which decreases hook and produces a rollout effect. Usually used only for ultrapower players. Ball's holes are drilled several inches to the left of the label for a right-handed player (or to the right of the label for a left-handed player) with an extra hole placed into the center of the top weight.

Back ends: Portion of the lane between the arrows and the pindeck which consists of softer wood (pine).

Back pitch: Angling of thumb hole backward so the tip of the thumb is extended away from the palm. It is used to help the thumb exit the ball sooner to maximize lift. By far the most common of the various thumb pitches.

Ball sanding: *See* Sanding.

Ball shining: *See* Shining.

Ball track: Portion of the ball that comes in contact with the lane as it rolls down the alley. (*See* Spinner, Semiroller, and Full roller.)

Blocked lane: A high-scoring condition whereby the boards closest to the gutters have very little lane conditioner and there is a heavy oil buildup on the center boards which helps to keep shots in the pocket. If too flagrant it is illegal.

Boards: Strips of wood that extend from the start of the approach to the pins. They are used as both a starting and an aiming point by players. There are 39 boards on a lane.

Carrydown: Movement of lane conditioner caused by a succession of shots from beyond where the oil was applied toward the pins. It decreases the ball's hooking on the backend.

Conditioner: *See* Oil.

Conventional grip: Placing one's fingers into the ball up to the second joint. It promotes accuracy but retards lift and striking power. Used primarily by beginning and less-advanced players.

Cranker: Bowler who relies more on a big hook and great carrying power than on accuracy to succeed.

Dots: Series of seven spots found seven feet past the foul line, on the foul line, and also at the two most common starting points on the approach. Each dot is on the same board as a corresponding arrow. Their primary function is to provide a reference point for foot placement. They can also be used for aiming points.

Early timing: Releasing the shot prior to having the sliding foot reach the foul line.

Fifth arrow: The third from the left (for a right-handed player) or from the right (when defined by a left-handed player) of the seven targets painted on the lane. Located on the 25th board.

Finger grips: Inserts placed into finger holes of the ball to promote later release for added lift.

Fingertip grip: Grip whereby the bowler inserts fingers only up to the first joint. Used to promote hook and striking power at the expense of some accuracy.

Finger weight: Drilling of the ball in such a manner that the finger holes are closer to the ball's label than is the thumb hole. It is a form of positive weight. Legal limit is one ounce.

First arrow: The farthest to the right (for a right-handed player) or from the left (when defined by a left-handed player) of the seven targets painted on the lane. Located on the fifth board.

Forward pitch: Angling of thumb hole inward and/or finger holes upward so the tip of the bowler's thumb is pointing toward the palm and/or the fingers are angled away from the palm. Used for players with small hands and/or short spans to help them grip the ball.

Fourth arrow: The target in the middle of the seven targets painted on the lane. Located on the 20th board.

Full roller: Method of rolling a ball in which the track area cuts between the thumb and finger holes. While it once was the shot most frequently used, it is rare among better players today because it lacks the carrying power of the more popular semiroller.

Heads: Front portion of the lane between the foul line and the arrows which consists of hard wood (maple).

Hold area: Amount of margin for error that is provided by an oil buildup in the center of the lane.

Hooking lanes: Dry or lightly oiled condition which causes maximum hook.

Kickbacks: Hard walls on both sides of the pin deck used to promote pin deflection so pins ricochet back into play. Also known as *sidewalls*.

Lane conditioner: *See* Oil.

Lateral pitch: Angling of thumb hole and/or finger holes to the left or to the right. Thumb pitch affects exit timing. Angling hole to the left for a right-handed player (or to the right for a left-handed bowler) delays thumb release from the ball, while angling to the opposite direction promotes earlier thumb exit. Improper lateral pitch can cause soreness of the thumb.

Late timing: So-called "plant-and-shoot" method whereby a player releases the shot after the sliding foot has come to a halt.

Leverage weight: Method of drilling the ball so that the holes are a few inches to the left of the label for a right-handed player (or to the right of the label for a left-handed bowler). Its effect is to make the ball skid longer and finish stronger. An extra hole is drilled in the opposite side of the ball. The center of the ball's weight block is thus located between the grip and the balance (extra) hole. The fourth hole is required to keep the weight differential within the legal limit of one ounce.

Lift: Power imparted to the ball's roll by the thumb exiting the ball first, followed by fingers, hitting through the shot on its release.

Limited distance dressing (LDD): *See* Short oil.

Loft: Distance the ball carries after it is released before it hits the lane. When properly executed the shot travels forward, *not* upward or downward.

Lofting: To loft one's shot.

Long oil: Condition in which oil is applied from the foul line to 35 or more feet of the 60-foot lane. Used primarily for PBA and other highly competitive tournaments to create a challenging condition for the advanced-level player.

Lustre King: Machine which applies wax to the surface of bowling balls to prolong ball life and decrease hook.

Maple: Hard wood used for that portion of the lane between the foul line and the arrows.

Negative weight: Use of one (or more) drilling methods that decreases the ball's amount of hook and/or gets the ball to end its skid and begin its roll pattern sooner. Primarily employed to combat long oil and/or heavily oiled lanes.

Oil: Conditioner applied to lane's surface that extends life of the alley while retarding ball hook.

Pin deck: Portion of the lane housing the pins.

Pine: Softer wood used for that portion of the lane between the arrows and the pin deck.

Pitch: Angle at which the holes are drilled.

Polyester: Substance used for bowling balls that was very popular among pros in the 1970s and remains commonly used by amateur players. Its effect is a cross between those of urethane and rubber. A polyester ball goes straighter and doesn't hit as well as a urethane ball but hooks more and hits harder than a rubber one. Preferred by advanced-level bowlers when the lanes are exceedingly dry.

Polyurethane: *See* Urethane.

Positive weight: Use of one (or more) in a series of drilling methods that decrease the ball's amount of hook and/or get it to conclude its skid and begin its roll pattern sooner. It is primarily employed to combat long oil and/or heavily oiled lanes.

Power player: *See* Cranker.

Reverse block: Extremely difficult lane condition in which the boards nearest the gutters are heavily oiled while the lane's center is relatively dry.

Reverse pitch: *See* Back pitch.

Revolutions: Barometer used to measure the number of times the bowling ball rolls over its circumference from when it is released until it reaches the pins. The greater the number, the more striking power usually results. Higher-quality amateur players and strokers usually achieve 10–20 revolutions. The PBA Tour's ultra-power players are usually in the 15–20 range on their strike shots.

Revs: *See* Revolutions.

Ringing 7-pin: Tap suffered by a left-handed player when the 4 pin flies around the 7 pin.

Ringing 10-pin: Tap suffered by a right-handed player when the 6 pin flies around the 10 pin.

Rollout: Malady in which ball uses up most of its impetus early on so little carrying power remains by the time it reaches the pins. The shot will actually stop its hooking pattern as it approaches the pins.

Rubber: Bowling ball surface which remains the most common among house balls. Rubber bowling balls were the balls of choice well into the 1970s until polyester balls were introduced. Rubber balls go straightest and may be useful for covering non-double-wood spares when decreasing hook is necessary on a very dry lane. Very rarely used by advanced players.

Sanding: Using an abrasive substance against the entire surface of the ball. Effect is to get ball to hook more.

Second arrow: The second from the right (for a right-handed player) or from the left (when defined by a left-handed player) of the seven targets painted on the lane. Located on the tenth board.

Semi-fingertip grip: Grip in which player inserts fingers into the ball halfway between the first and second joints.

Semiroller: Most popular shot among better-quality players in which the ball's track area can be found just outside of the thumb and finger holes.

Seventh arrow: The farthest to the left (for a right-handed player) or from the right (when defined by a left-handed player) of the seven targets painted on the lane. Located on the 35th board.

Shining: Adding wax to ball's surface to make it smoother. Used to retard hook and/or extend ball life.

Short oil: Also known as *limited distance dressing* (or LDD). Condition in which oil is applied to the front 24 feet (or less) of the lane, thus leaving the final 36 feet (or more) dry.

Shur-Hook: Cork substance used in thumb hole to promote better grip. Commonly used by the player who wants to maintain a similar feel when switching bowling balls.

Sidewalls: Walls to either side of the pin deck off of which pins can ricochet back into play. Also known as *kickbacks*.

Sixth arrow: The second from the left (for a right-handed player) or from the right (when defined by a left-handed player) of the seven targets painted on the lane. Located on the 30th board.

Soft 7-pin: Shot by a left-handed player on which the 7 pin remains as the 4 pin falls weakly into the gutter. Caused by the ball deflecting to the left after colliding with the headpin.

Soft 10-pin: Shot by a right-handed player on which the 10 pin remains as the 6 pin falls weakly into the gutter. Caused by the ball deflecting to the right after it collides with the headpin.

Solid 7-pin: *See* Ringing 7-pin.

Solid 10-pin: *See* Ringing 10-pin.

Spinner: Method of delivering a shot so that only the small portion of the ball (around the 7 o-clock position for right-handers and 5 o'clock for lefties) is in contact with the lane. As a rule this is not a very successful shot for maximizing carrying power and thus is rarely employed by the better-quality bowler.

Stroker: Player who relies more on accuracy than power. Usually noted for having a "by the book" style that includes smooth movements, remaining square to the target throughout the delivery, and being on time at the foul line.

Swing area: Amount of margin for error to the right of a right-handed player's target (or to the left of a left-handed player's target) that is provided by a lack of conditioner on the lowest numbered boards.

Third arrow: The third from the right (for a right-handed player) or from the left (when defined by a left-handed player) of the seven targets painted on the lane. Located on the 15th board.

Three-quarter roller: *See* Semiroller.

Thumb weight: Method of drilling ball so the thumb hole is closer to the label than are the finger holes. It is a form of negative weight that causes the ball to roll sooner. Maximum legal limit is one ounce.

Tight lanes: Heavy and/or long oil pattern that retards a shot's hook.

Timing: Relationship between the sliding foot and the hand that releases the shot. (*See* Early timing and Late timing.)

Thumb grips: Inserts placed inside of thumb hole to help player get a better grip. Used primarily to maintain the same feel when player switches bowling balls.

Top weight: Drilling of ball so that there is up to maximum legally allowed limit of three ounces more of weight above the label than there is below it. Effect on shot is similar to positive weight.

Track: *See* Ball track.

Tweener: Style of bowling that combines some of the power of the cranker with some of the style and accuracy of the stroker.

Urethane: Surface substance introduced in bowling balls in early 1980s. Considered state-of-the-art equipment that is noted for its superior gripping of the lane coupled with maximum carrying power.

Walled lane: *See* Blocked Lane.

Walls: *See* Kickbacks.

Weight block: Added section of weight on the inside of the ball. Can be used to maximum advantage by skilled ball driller when placed off center. (*See* Axis weight, Back pitch, Finger weight, Forward pitch, Lateral pitch, Leverage weight, Negative weight, Positive weight, Thumb weight, and Top weight.)

Washout: Spare leave involving the headpin (and possibly other pins to its left) in combination with the 10 pin (for right-handed players) or the headpin (and possibly other pins to its right) in combination with the 7 pin (for left-handed players). Not considered a split.

APPENDIX B

BOWLING BALL MANUFACTURERS

Arranged in Alphabetical Order by Manufacturer

MANUFACTURER	TOP NAME BALL	STAFF MEMBERS
AMF	Angle	Tom Baker, Joe Berardi, Frank Ellenburg, Mats Karlsson, Betty Morris, Jimmie Pritts, Cheryl Robinson, Jay Robinson, Brian Voss, Leila Wagner, Dick Weber, and Pete Weber.
Brunswick	Rhino	Parker Bohn, Cindy Coburn, Dave Davis, Amleto Monacelli, Virgina Norton, Randy Pedersen, Johnny Petraglia, Mark Roth, Judy Soutar, Barbara Thorberg, Kent Wagner, Lisa Wagner, and Mark Williams.
Columbia	U-Dot	Mark Baker, George Branham, Tom Crites, Scott Devers, Dave Ferraro, Bob Handley, Marshall Holman, Dave Husted, David Ozio, Ron Palombi, Teata Semiz, Rick Steelsmith, and Tony Westlake.
Ebonite	Thunderbolt	Earl Anthony, Leanne Barrette, Jeanne Maiden, Aleta Sill, and Walter Ray Williams.
Faball	Hammer	Steve Cook.
Track	Enforcer	Ted Hannahs and Steve Wunderlich.

BOWLING BALL GUIDE

The following information is provided as a rough guide to the wide variety of equipment that is available to today's bowler. The information on specific balls has been supplied by their manufacturers.

As a general rule, if you wish to invest in one urethane ball, select one that is suited for "Most" or "Medium oil" lane conditions. However, if you are a cranker who wants to decrease your very large natural hook you will want a ball that is designed to roll more straight (one that has a higher hardness number and is meant for dry lanes). Conversely, if you are a stroker who wishes to maximize your ball's hook, pick a softer-shelled ball (a lower number hardness rating) that is meant for oily lanes.

If you plan on buying two urethane balls, the chances are that you should pick one toward either end of the spectrum (i.e., one for drier conditions and another for more oily lanes).

Keep in mind that the highly competitive ball-manufacturing market is forever changing as the major companies seek to produce a product that is superior to those of their rivals. As such, the information we have provided is the most up-to-date as of publication. For more information, see your local pro.

BALL/COLOR (MANUFACTURER)	TYPE/ HARDNESS	WEIGHTS	CHARACTERISTICS	CONDITION
Angle/Purple (AMF)	Urethane/76–78	12, 14–16	Can be polished to reduce hook.	Heavy oil.
Angle Plus/Black (AMF)	Urethane/77–80	12–16	Exceptional hook on long oil. Solid strike core for less deflection.	Medium and long oil.
Angle/Black (AMF)	Urethane/77–79	12–16	Longer slide before it starts to roll.	Most.
Angle/Blue (AMF)	Urethane/76–79	12, 14–16	Sanded finish gives more back end hook.	Oily heads.
Angle LD/Many (AMF)	Urethane/78–81	12, 14–16	Cuts through heavy head oil for hook at back end. Good spare ball.	Short oil.
Pro Classic/Black (AMF)	Rubber/80+	10, 12, 14–16	Three-dot guidance system to follow line to pins. General purpose ball.	Most.
Questar/Many (AMF)	Plastic/80+	6, 8, 10, 12, 14–16	Eye-catching patterns.	Most.

Ball (Manufacturer)	Material/Hardness	Weights	Description	Lane Conditions
Rhino/Black (Brunswick)	Urethane/78–81	12, 14–16	All Rhinos feature process-integrated weight block that is chemically bonded to the ball's core.	Medium to dry lanes.
Rhino/Wine (Brunswick)	Urethane/78–81	12, 14–16	All Rhinos designed to help keep pin trajectory low.	Oily.
Rhino/Blue (Brunswick)	Urethane/78–81	12, 14–16	See "Rhino/Black" and "Rhino/Wine."	Medium to oily.
Rhino/ Cobalt (Brunswick)	Urethane/78–81	12, 14–16	See "Rhino/Black" and "Rhino/Wine."	Heavy oil.
Rhino/Black Pearl (Brunswick)	Urethane/78–81	12, 14–16	See "Rhino/Black" and "Rhino/Wine."	Dry.
Vector II/Blue (Columbia)	Urethane/76–78	14–16	Designed for low-track players. Advanced weight block produces maximum number of revs.	Slick heads, pines, and back ends.
Vector I/Black (Columbia)	Urethane/76–78	14–16	Increases revs. Low center of gravity aids carry.	Slick heads and pines; medium back ends.
U-Dot/Black (Columbia)	Urethane/76–78	10–16	Can be polished for dryer conditions.	Slick heads, medium pines, and dry to medium back ends.
U—Dot/Wine (Columbia)	Urethane/78–80	10–16	Mid-range hooking ball makes it versatile.	Most.

BOWLING BALL GUIDE (continued)

BALL/COLOR (MANUFACTURER)	TYPE/HARDNESS	WEIGHTS	CHARACTERISTICS	CONDITION
U—Dot/Slate (Columbia)	Urethane/80–82	10–16	Formulated to retain its ability to combat LDD.	Short oil.
Yellow Dot/Maroon (Columbia)	Polyester/76–78	10–16	Made for bowler who wishes to carry only one polyester ball.	Medium heads with dry to medium pines and dry back ends.
White Dot/Many (Columbia)	Polyester/78–80	10–16	Ideal for conditions that hook too much for urethane.	Medium heads with dry pines and dry back ends.
Thunderbolt/Black (Ebonite)	Urethane/76	14–16	Longer roll and sharp hook lessen deflection to aid carry.	Heavy oil.
Thunderbolt M/D/Grey (Ebonite)	Urethane/76–78	14–16	Dynamically balanced power core.	Medium to dry.
Firebolt/Black (Ebonite)	Urethane/76	12, 14–16	Shiny finish made for average lane condition.	Medium to dry.
Firebolt II/Blue/Black (Ebonite)	Urethane/76	14–16	Formulated to avoid rollout, even on very oily lanes.	Heavy oil.
Gyro I/Blue/Grey (Ebonite)	Urethane/78	10, 12–16	Very low price for a urethane ball. High-density weight block.	Heavy oil.
Gyro I/Jade (Ebonite)	Urethane/78–80	10, 12–16	Very low price for a urethane ball. High-density weight block.	Medium to dry.

Ball/Manufacturer	Shell/Hardness	Weights	Description	Lane Condition
Lady Ebonite/Many (Ebonite)	Urethane/77	10–16	Designed for women bowlers. Smooth roll and predictable hook. Very low price for a urethane ball.	Medium to dry.
Hammer/Blue (Faball)	Urethane/76–77	13–16	Strong back-end reaction.	Medium to heavy oil.
Hammer/Red (Faball)	Urethane/75–76	13–16	Less back-end hook than Blue Hammer. Exceptional carry.	Medium oil.
Hammer/Black (Faball)	Urethane/77–78	13–16	Slightly less back-end hook than Red Hammer.	Medium to light oil.
Hammer/Red Pearl (Faball)	Urethane/77–78	13–16	Moderate back-end reaction. Designed for dry heads.	Dry to light oil.
Hammer/Blue Pearl (Faball)	Urethane/77–78	13–16	Slightly less back-end reaction than Red Pearl. Also made for dry heads.	Dry to light oil.
Nail/Blue (Faball)	Urethane/81–83	13–16	Goes through heads very well. Exceptional carry. Keep polished for best results.	Dry lanes.
Enforcer/Black (Track)	Urethane/77–78	14–16	Dual weight blocks. Very thick shell. Can be drilled 26 ways to adapt to any lane condition. Skids longer than Blue Enforcer.	Medium to dry.
Enforcer/Blue (Track)	Urethane/75–76	14–16	See top three items under "Enforcer/Black." Has massive back-end hooking ability.	Oily lanes.
Enforcer/Burgundy (Track)	Urethane/79–82	14–16	See top three items under "Enforcer/Black."	Dry or short oil.
Track 10 Blue (Track)	Urethane/75–76	14–16	Hooks most of entire line of Track balls. Dense, low weight block enhances early roll.	Oily lanes.
Trackster/Many (Track)	Urethane/78–80	10–16	Standard pancake weight block. Attractive colors.	Dry lanes.

APPENDIX C

Bowling Resources

American Bowling Congress/*Bowling* Magazine
5301 South 76th Street
Greendale, Wisconsin 53129
(414) 421-6400

Billiard and Bowling Institute of America
200 Castlewood
North Palm Beach, Florida 33408
(305) 842-4100

Bowlers Journal
101 East Erie Street
Chicago, Illinois 60611
(312) 266-7171

Bowling Digest
The Century Building
990 Grove Street
Evanston, Illinois 60201
(312) 491-6440

Bowling Proprieters Association of America
615 Six Flags Drive
Arlington, Texas 76011
(817) 460-2121

Bowling Writers Association of America
6357 Siena Street
Centerville, Ohio 45459
(513) 433-5988

Federation Internationale des Quilleurs (FIQ)
Linnustajantie 6 1 49
02940 Espoo 94
Finland

Ladies Professional Bowlers Tour
7171 Cherryvale Blvd.
Rockford, Illinois 61112
(815) 332-5756

National Bowling Council
1919 Pennsylvania Avenue NW
Washington, D.C. 20006
(202) 659-9070

National Bowling Hall of Fame and Museum
111 Stadium Plaza
St. Louis, Missouri 63120
(314) 231-6340

Professional Bowlers Association
1720 Merriman Road, PO Box 5118
Akron, Ohio 44313
(216) 836-5568

Women's International Bowling Congress
5301 South 76th Street
Greendale, Wisconsin 53129
(414) 421-9000

Young American Bowling Alliance
5301 South 76th Street
Greendale, Wisconsin 53129
(414) 421-4700

ABOUT THE AUTHORS

The Aulby File

June 1979
As a rookie he won a triple crown event, the PBA National Championship, as he beat all-time great Earl Anthony in the title game, 245–217.

December 1979
Aulby was named the PBA's Rookie of the Year.

1980
Won two more titles: the Midas Open and the Tucson Open. Was the Tour's leading money winner among left-handed players and ranked third overall with $86,735.

1981
For the second consecutive year he finished among the top 10 earners as he claimed his fourth national title.

October 1984
He ended a three-year winless streak in dramatic fashion by emerging victorious in front of his

hometown fans during the
Indianapolis Open.

November 1984   Only three weeks after his Indy
triumph, Aulby captured another of
bowling's most coveted events, the
Brunswick World Open. In the title
game Aulby outscored veteran Gary
Skidmore, 253–241, after having
previously eliminated Marshall
Holman, 241–212.

December 1984   Aulby concluded the year with
$110,620 to again pace all PBA
southpaws (fourth overall).

1985   Aulby's dream year. He won five
titles en route to becoming the first
PBA performer to top the $200,000
barrier in a single year. For his
efforts he was named both Player
and Bowler of the Year as he
became the only man to capture
those awards and to have also been
honored as the PBA's Rookie of the
Year.

June 1986   Mike and brother-in-law Steve Cook
successfully defended their doubles
title in Las Vegas.

December 1986   For the fifth time in seven years he
finished among the PBA's top 10 in
official earnings.

March 1988   Aulby rolled back-to-back games of
233 and 249 in the championship
round to win the Miller Lite Open.

March 1989   He overcame a late 20-pin deficit by
doubling in the tenth frame to win

his 15th national title as he took the Showboat Atlantic City Open by defeating three opponents.

March 1989

Aulby became the first southpaw since Earl Anthony (in 1981) to win consecutive crowns. His overpowering performance at the Budweiser Open included a 243.1 weekly average that was nearly eight full pins superior to his nearest rival. In the title game Aulby routed Brad Snell, 246–202.

April 1989

He captured the second of three jewels in bowling's triple crown by winning the U. S. Open. En route to the title he defeated all but seven of 26 opponents in match play. By month's end he had shattered the PBA record for earnings during the Winter Tour with $194,555.

May 1989

He captured the American Bowling Congress Bud Light Masters by defeating Mike Edwards in the title game, 211–207. Aulby's fourth 1989 triumph was worth $43,600. It enabled him to reclaim the record for single-year earnings that he had held since 1985.

The Ferraro File

1983-1984   He was a part-time player on the national tour with modest success.

July 1985   He set an unwanted PBA title round record for rolling the highest score in a losing cause. Dave produced 11 strikes—leaving only the 4-7 spare in the ninth frame—but still dropped the semi-final game of the Austin Open to Mark Baker, 279-278.

December 1985   Since deciding to roll his shots more directly to the pocket he improved significantly. Finished the year 40th in earnings.

November 1986   Ferraro entered the title round as the top seed of the Budweiser Classic in search of his first win on the National Tour. He started the title game with six consecutive strikes as he defeated former Rookie of the Year John Gant, 254-221.

December 1986   He moved up to 23rd on earnings list with year-end career high total of $56,208.

March 1987   He enhanced his ever-improving reputation as a superb performer under pressure as he doubled in the final frame of the title game of the Miller Lite Open. Ferraro's victim was Brian Voss in a thrilling 211-204 match.

December 1987   In a remarkably consistent year, Ferraro cashed in 24 of 28 national tournaments. He posted the Tour's third highest average (215.27) and finished tenth in earnings with yet another career high, $95,023.

June 1988

He combined with fellow New Yorker Joe Berardi to win Aulby and Cook's favorite event, the Showboat Doubles Classic in Las Vegas. The winning duo beat Brian Voss and Pete Weber in the championship match.

September 1988

Ferraro and Voss clashed heads again, this time in Canada in the title game of the Tour's only match play event, the PBA #7 Invitational. Having averaged a stunning 257.3 in eliminating Randy Rose, Marshall Holman, and Mats Karlsson, Ferraro disposed of 1988's top performer, Voss, 210–204.

December 1988

Ferraro beat former Player of the Year Walter Ray Williams to win the prestigious Touring Players Championship. Ferraro was named to the American Bowling Congress' first unit All-America team after becoming only the 10th man in PBA history to earn over $150,000 ($150,395) in one year.

March 1989

He came within a hair of doubling in the tenth frame in an unsuccessful effort to claim his first "major" title as he finished second to Pete Weber in the PBA National Championship.

INDEX